W9-ANQ-346

Blues

a photographic documentary

Blues

a photographic documentary

david harrison

CRESCENT BOOKS

NEW YORK

Blues – A Photographic Documentary

This 1997 edition published by Crescent Books,
a division of Random House Value Publishing,
201 East 50th Street, New York, NY 10022.
http://www.randomhouse.com

Random House
New York ● Toronto ● London ● Sydney ● Auckland

A CIP catalog record for this book is available from the
Library of Congress

Copyright © 1997 Studio

All rights reserved. This publication may not be
reproduced, stored in a retrieval system or
transmitted, in any form or by any means, electronic,
mechanical, photocopying or otherwise, without the
prior written permission of the publishers.

ISBN 0-517-14158-2
Printed and bound in Singapore
10, 9, 8, 7, 6, 5, 4, 3, 2, 1

For Becky, Corin and Laura – again

OPPOSITE TITLE PAGE
Otis Rush came out of Chicago's West Side,
with Buddy Guy and Magic Sam, and with a
new sound that combined tortured vocals with
fleet-fingered guitar. With a few exceptions, his
early records are moody classics of their kind,
but he has never realized his full potential since.
He is pictured here at the 1969 Ann Arbor Blues
Festival, at the height of his powers, but he
remains a formidable performer.
PHOTOGRAPH: DOUG FULTON

acknowledgements

The publishers wish to thank the following sources for supplying the photographs.
Please note that the photographs are copyright and reproduction is strictly
prohibited without prior permission from the copyright holder. See captions for
photographer credits.

Blues Unlimited: Parker A. Dinkins/John Holley/David Hawkins Studio/
Courtesy Bobo Jenkins/Terry Johnson/Gerhard Robs/Courtesy Mike Rowe/
Frank Scott/Chris Strachwitz/Courtesy Gayle Dean Wardlow
Terry Cryer
David Evans Collection/David Evans
Doug Fulton
Bill Greensmith
Axel Küstner
Dave Peabody
Photo Reserve: Paul Natkin
Sylvia Pitcher Photo Library: Sylvia Pitcher/Brian Smith/Frank Weston
Kevin Reynolds
Stagefright Photography: Marc Marnie
The Weston Collection
Val Wilmer

Thanks are also due to *Folk Roots* magazine for use of some material which first
appeared in the magazine, and to *Blueprint* magazine.

contents

introduction

If music is an international language, then the blues is the Esperanto of music. The blues probably originated in Mississippi of uncertain parentage, grew up in the cotton fields of the south and the slums of the north, and is now a citizen of the world. Everywhere that western popular music is played, you can hear the blues in one form or another, and in each of the diverse strands that make up western music. The blues is the bedrock of popular music, an extraordinary rise to fame for a child of poverty and depression.

This book is a celebration of the blues through the printed page. Accept that words can only guide and suggest and chronicle, and that pictures are a frozen moment in time – a moment that may not even be typical. That doesn't matter: the music is still there for all to hear, and in a profusion that the early blues singers would find totally baffling. But even so, books and magazines can add to the value of the music, by showing how and why it developed, why it is so important, and what the owners of those voices preserved on ancient wax or modern CD look(ed) like. A good photograph, such as those presented here, can flesh out the sound of the blues in a visual way – give a personality and a face to a shadowy sonic image from a remote time and place. It's all part of the celebration of a music coming up to a century old and looking as young as ever.

These days, there are blues singers and bands in every country that has access to American music. Musicians whose first language is far removed from English, let alone backwoods Mississippi, have taken up the insistent rhythms and core subjects of the blues – sex, money, unemployment, poverty – and added their own particular flavour. The best far transcend mere copies; the worst – where Birmingham, England, merely apes Birmingham, Alabama – at least serve to remind us that the blues may have come out of Africa generations ago, but they are often equally strongly influenced by the white country music of the European settlers – and that in itself has echoes of every country that sent emigrants to the New World. There's a pleasing feeling of the wheel coming full circle in the music of Mali's Ali Farka Touré, whose big influence was the hypnotic blues of John Lee Hooker, yet the droning, primitive sound of One String Sam could still be heard on the Detroit streets as late as 1956, and the African fife-and-drum sound was a regular feature of dances in the Mississippi hill country right up to the seventies, and probably later.

There are European blues bands, blues singers from Australia, classical composers inspired

Sleepy John Estes sounded old even when he was young, so when Bill Broonzy claimed he was dead, everyone believed him. Then, in 1962, Estes was discovered in Brownsville, Tennessee – blind and in terrible poverty, but sounding as unique and archaic as ever. His strange, crying vocals, understated guitar and incredibly personal songs were heard at festivals and on records all over the world before his death in 1977. He is pictured with mandolinist Yank Rachell, with whom he first recorded in 1929.

PHOTOGRAPH: SYLVIA PITCHER

by the blues, a string quartet that plays the blues, and innumerable rock groups with the blues underpinning everything they do. Muddy Waters, whose own career spanned impeccable country blues to the edges of electric rock, claimed that rock 'n' roll was the baby of the blues. That is self evident, but more interesting is the way that the blues have taken some of the youthful energy and insistent rhythms of both rock and its sister, soul, to keep itself alive and relevant to a new generation. It's difficult to see the joins sometimes in the work of singers like Robert Cray and Joe Louis Walker, but the blues' roots are always there.

The blues has travelled a long way, and along the way it has had affairs with jazz, pop, ballads, boogie woogie, country and western, and gospel. But although the photographs in this book concentrate on the singers after the Second World War, any understanding of the music must start in the twenties, in places like Mississippi, Memphis, Dallas — and Atlanta, Georgia.

The city of Atlanta rises from the pine woods and rich, red soil of Georgia like some megalithic monument. Snuggling around the edges are prosperous, wooded suburbs seeking shelter from the muggy humidity, but the downtown business area is a Legoland of skyscrapers which at least try to distance themselves from the traditional slab.

This is *Gone With the Wind* country. Margaret Mitchell, creator of feckless Scarlett O'Hara and Rhett Butler who frankly couldn't give a damn, lies in sprawling Oakland cemetery, near Little Lizzie who, in 1856, 'budded on earth and bloomed in Heaven'. Not far away, by the side of the elevated Rapid Transport system, is a bleak, characterless highway called Decatur Street, that forms one boundary of the black district of Atlanta. There are no walls, no fences, no signs; but it was between here and Auburn Avenue that the majority of rural blacks settled in the years between the two world wars.

In just 30 years, Atlanta's population doubled, as the cotton industry tottered and poor agricultural practices pushed many farmers towards bankruptcy. The Yankee General Sherman burned old Atlanta in 1864, an act of war still recalled, more than a century later, with bitterness and the defiant flying of the Confederacy flag. The new Atlanta, an unlovely, sprawling place, seemed to grow haphazardly and with little control.

In the inter-war years, that area between Decatur and Auburn had the worst houses in the city, the highest rate of crime and poverty, and the largest number of unemployed. The Ku Klux Klan prowled outside, burning crosses — and lynching those who failed to keep their Klan-ordained place — on Stone Mountain. It's no coincidence that the Reverend Martin Luther King is buried on an island in the centre of an artificial lake in Auburn Avenue, among the people for whom he dreamed a dream. Even so, the luxury of the Martin Luther King Jr. Center for Non Violent Change, with its T-shirts, records, posters and mugs, seems to fit uneasily among the faded wooden houses on brick stilts of the poor black neighbourhood, a district that has changed little since the days when the blues first came to Atlanta.

Bailey's 81 Theater was situated on Decatur Street, and most of the major black touring shows stopped there in the twenties. Gertrude Ma Rainey, magisterial Mother of the Blues, moaned her blues at Bailey's, and Bessie Smith, with the voice of a fallen black angel, dazzled audiences there.

'Down in Atlanta, Georgia, under the viaduct every day, drinkin' corn and hollerin' hooray, pianos playing' til' the break of day', she sang in 'Preaching the Blues', and if it was difficult to imagine the elegant Bessie of Carl van Vechten's sophisticated photographs knocking back the

Maxwell Street in Chicago was the scene of a market where many blues singers could be found playing and entertaining the shoppers. Some, like Little Walter and Big John Wrencher, were lucky enough to record; others, like Little Pat Rushing (pictured here in 1978, just off Maxwell Street), never struck lucky.

PHOTOGRAPH: FRANK WESTON

booze in a street corner joint – well, she was a hard woman underneath the glamour, and her audiences understood just what she was singing about.

There were dance halls and clubs on Magnolia Street and Peachtree, house parties and illegal drinking dens everywhere that people gathered. All provided employment for the travelling bluesmen, for whom Atlanta was one of the main gathering places.

Blues comes from an oppressed culture that outsiders can try to understand, and sometimes try to recreate with a white middle-class earnestness, but never really live. Blues is the soul of the black American enshrined in music – not, as is popularly supposed, just bitterness and sorrow, but also joy in the rhythms of the dance, and the pleasures of sex and drink and gambling, the simple delights of nonsensical hokum singalongs. Entire books have been devoted to interpreting the lyrics of blues, and that is part of that filtering process. The listeners for whom those blues were written helped invent those curious figures of speech. They knew about black heroes ('Gonna ride like Stavin' Chain') and Tom Moore, the farmer now immortalized in a small way in a bitter blues by Lightnin' Hopkins. They understood the significance of Highway 61 and the mojo and the number 4-11-44. Blues reflected their lives and experiences; others can listen and grow to love the music, borrow it for a while, but it must remain, at heart, the property of its creators.

So if collectors get misty eyed over the thought of Atlanta in the twenties, with Peg Leg Howell's raucous Gang making a glorious racket in Decatur Street, Barbecue Bob whaling his 12-string for patrons of a barbecue joint in the suburb of Buckhead, dances accompanied by Curly Weaver and tragic Eddie Mapp, or street entertainment by the incomparable Blind Willie McTell, it's as well to weigh up everything that went with the early blues as well.

Decatur Street is best experienced through a magnificent dance number named after it in 1933 by the Georgia Browns (Curly Weaver, Buddy Moss, Fred McMullen), rather than walking the amorphous thoroughfare it is today. Happily, Auburn is still in a time warp, an extraordinary street full of storefront African Baptist churches and black bars leading from the King Center up to Woodruff Park and the Atlanta business area.

In 1987, I walked Auburn from the King Center to an hotel on Peachtree Street that was in another world. Residents and loungers were polite, willing to chat, fascinated by a British accent, and more interested in my camera than in talking about the blues. None, even the older ones, had heard of any of the old-time blues singers, although they pointed me to a blues club called Blind Willie's. Blind Willie who? They weren't sure.

Later, I met some of the Atlanta Symphony Orchestra and chorus. Not one was even vaguely aware that Atlanta had been one of the major pre-war recording centres for blues, and that Willie McTell had still been recording as late as 1956. These people, who specialized in the European symphonic and choral tradition, had no conception of the wealth of music created by their own black neighbours – but as their black neighbours had little interest in their own traditions, why should the privileged whites? And how many educated people in any country have any conception of their own folk traditions, let alone the legacy of a people who remain an embarrassing indictment of a brutal and violent past they would rather forget?

The blues is a reminder of that past, too, which is probably why the black community prefers Stax and Motown, Diana Ross and Stevie Wonder, James Brown and Michael Jackson: they are the achievers, the winners. As pointed out earlier, the best modern bluesmen, such as Robert Cray, owe more to soul and rock 'n' roll and gospel than the vibrant folk music of Barbecue Bob and Blind Willie McTell. I only heard one musician on Auburn – a guitarist playing through an open window. He was running through The Beatles' 'Hey Jude'.

The sheer romance of standing where semi-legendary figures like Blind Willie and Peg Leg Howell had once played was rather overwhelming. It was like unexpectedly coming across Dante's tomb in a side street in Ravenna, or realizing in a Portuguese cathedral that beneath the sepulchre against which I was resting lay Vasco da Gama, who changed history by finding a sea route to India.

Auburn Avenue has the same effect on anyone who loves the blues, and there is more of a sense of history pervading old Auburn than you will find in Beale Street in Memphis or in the French Quarter of New Orleans.

A place such as Auburn transcends its own physical nature by association, romantic or otherwise.

Surprisingly, perhaps, Auburn is listed in the Atlanta Convention and Visitors' Bureau guide under what is now called the Martin Luther King Jr. Historic Site. That includes much of the old blues heartland – or, as the guide euphemistically puts it, 'the historic buildings and store fronts in the surrounding blocks of Sweet Auburn Avenue'.

These are being restored to the way they looked at the turn of the century, 'when the street was the economic heart of black Atlanta'. There's a grim irony in the thought of the streets around Auburn having enough of a legitimate economy to have any kind of heart, but it's good that the places where Willie McTell, Laughing Charley Lincoln, Barbecue Bob Hicks and Peg Leg Howell once performed will not vanish like their music.

One day I went to Madison, a remarkably well-preserved slice of the Old South, with streets of gingerbread mansions, complete with pillared verandahs, porches and rocking chairs. As a favour to its senator, who was a pre-war friend, Sherman didn't burn it as he marched through Georgia. Street singer Peg Leg Howell came from Madison – although, as the old lady recalled, blacks weren't allowed within the town boundary after dark. She'd never heard of Howell, or any kind of black music, although she was quite happy to point out the spot where the slave quarters used to be. Madison is an historical place, but its memories are very selective.

A few months earlier, on the other side of the continent, the Louis Madison All Stars were playing in Lord Jim's, a Victorian-style bar in San Francisco that glittered with decorated mirrors, barley-sugar brass and polished mahogany counters. It was a bit off the usual tourist trail, an occasion for enormous strawberry daiquiris on the house and a chance to drink with the band.

The All Stars were a mixed-race band – black musicians, but a white vocalist, Vicki Jo Coleman, who knew just what to do with songs by Koko Taylor, Janis Joplin and Willie Dixon. Madison himself was a former James Brown sideman, and claimed to have written 'Please Please Please' for him, while guitarist David Workman had worked with Muddy Waters, Howlin' Wolf and many other big-name Chicago stars.

The band played for pleasure – lots of swinging, rhythmic dance numbers, the odd Stax soul song, and heartfelt slow numbers from Vicki Jo. Both Madison and Workman seemed delighted that someone, a foreign someone even, was interested in talking about the music and the people, and that they had actually heard of Muddy and Wolf. The American patrons just got on with their drinking and talking, and simply increased the volume when the band started to play. Yet again, just like those Georgians and most civilized people, Californians were ignoring what blues lovers from the rest of the world would pay hard-earned money to hear, live, on its own home ground. Standard club behaviour, shrugged Vicki Jo. That's what they expected. That's what happened everywhere.

Another year, many thousands of miles and a world of difference away in Europe: Son House, Bukka White and Skip James were in town.

The blues is (or was in the sixties) a young enough music for the first generation of practitioners to be both alive and occasionally active, albeit a little rusty and hesitant. European blues collectors were astounded they were still living – and for their part the artists were equally amazed that anyone still wanted to hear their old-time music after decades of being forgotten and the onslaught of electric blues and rock 'n' roll. As pointed out earlier, America, like most other countries, is very careless with its musical heritage.

But somehow, miraculously, Son House – one of the most revered of all bluesmen; the ferocious voice and stinging slide guitar on four poorly recorded records from 1930; Son House, who had played with the great Charley Patton himself; Son House, who came from Mississippi where, as everyone then was convinced, all the great blues originated; yes, *that* Son House – was in Europe. Since those early days, of course, more of both his 1930 session and the forties Library of Congress recordings have surfaced, and Son House can now be seen in the context of his contemporaries, rather than in isolated splendour; but for European blues fans, it was akin to King Oliver and Johnny Dodds turning up unexpectedly at a Chris Barber date.

Not only Son House, but also Skip James – possibly the most eccentric and uniquely gifted of all the early bluesmen – and Bukka White, whose 'Fixin' to Die' became something of a sixties festival anthem.

And all three from Mississippi, which proved what was generally felt – that anyone from anywhere else (Memphis was just about acceptable) wasn't a real, dyed-in-the-wool, authentic blues singer. Those were years of exploration, discovery and anticipation, both inside and outside America; but also, in retrospect, considerable naivety.

When Muddy Waters brought a full-blooded Chicago blues band, complete with amplification, over to Europe, an awful lot of listeners felt he had sold out to rock 'n' roll. But how were they to know that the blues listened to by black Americans was now plugged in and electric when acoustic Big Bill Broonzy, in the twilight of his career, was billed as the last great blues singer, and relished it?

It was all a bit baffling. If Big Bill was the last, then what were House, James and White doing here? Where did other visitors, with curious names like Big Joe Williams, Lightnin' Hopkins, Sleepy John Estes, John Henry Barbee and Howlin' Wolf, fit in to all this? It wasn't too long, thanks to magazines such as *Blues Unlimited* and *Blues World*, small record companies, such as OJL, Folkways, Arhoolie, Kokomo, PWB, Matchbox and Roots, and dedicated researchers, like Paul Oliver, Chris Strachwitz, Bruce Bastin, Jacques Demetres, Sam Charters and Gayle Dean Wardlow, before the truth began to struggle, painfully, to the surface from where it had been buried beneath a mountain of complete indifference.

Son House seemed curiously unassuming for such a giant. He wore a sort of Fair Isle cardigan which seemed awfully cosy and suburban for a great bluesman from Mississippi, and was so frail he had to be helped on to the stage. He didn't seem at all fazed by a 2,000-seat concert hall, and smiled quietly and said nothing as he was handed a metal-bodied guitar. A moment's concentration, a quick slide down the neck, and all those old Paramount 78s, with their crackly surfaces and constricted sound, came to life in front of us. The voice was deeper (although God knows what he really sounded like in 1930, before Paramount's low-fi shambles filtered his vocal chords through mush) and the slashing slide-guitar figures more hesitant. But he was an old man, some 20 years past his peak and long retired – until American collectors tracked him down – and his performance had to be accepted on that level. But if the technical brilliance had diminished, the intensity of approach hadn't, and as he warmed up, so the guitar work became more fluid, and the slide stabbed the music with percussive body blows to counterpoint the fragmentary melodies

People all over the world have heard of this unlovely street, one of the few lifted out of grim reality by song. This is Beale Street, Memphis, subject of countless blues and once the thriving but violent heart of black night life. 'A rough, tough, gambling, whoring, cutting, musical, living street', as researcher Bengt Olsson memorably called it. The heyday of Beale Street was in the twenties and thirties; these days it is just a tourist attraction.

PHOTOGRAPH: SYLVIA PITCHER

carried by the rich, worn voice. Those hard-edged Mississippi vocals, so fierce and uncompromising, had a directness and passion which few Europeans had experienced live before. Nothing that House recorded after his discovery even hinted at the sheer grandeur of the man in action, or the astonishing contrast between the old age pensioner on stage and the aggressive, pungently dynamic music emanating from such a small figure.

Skip James was more introvert. He didn't hunch over his guitar like House, but his music was more inward looking, with less surface brilliance. He seemed to sing more for himself than for us, but that curious high voice sounded closer to his 1931 recordings than House achieved. He was also an enormously complex character with strange drives, as his biography amply demonstrates, but his bitterness with the breaks life had given him seemed self evident, even when he was being fêted in a European concert hall. He didn't come across as someone with whom you could enjoy leaning on a bar; his songs are unremittingly gloomy and devil-ridden, and if his 78s were the only ones to have survived, the myth of the blues as a depressing music would have been fully justified. Between House's almost religious fervour and Bukka White's rhythmic chronicles of prison and death, Skip James remains in the memory as a bleak, lonely figure, whose music was all he was willing to give away.

Bukka White was a big, burly man, much more of an extrovert who was confident in his own ability and knew he deserved to be there. His shimmering slide guitar was very different from Son House's – where House used the whine to punctuate, emphasize and underline in a gospel frenzy, Bukka White's danced. It carried the sound of the Southern trains, of the hunting dogs, of Saturday night juke joints. Son House's singing was anguished, pain filled, uncomfortable. Skip James was remote, dispassionate, brooding. Bukka White's songs were obsessed with prison, illness and death, and his music was thematically limited – but that means little in any folk music, particularly the blues. That harsh, strained voice ringing against those relentless, rhythmic bottleneck (actually, a metal ring) figures opened a window to a place and a time and a vision of life that was as alien to us as the Burundi drummers, Japanese Noh theatre, or a Balinese gamelan orchestra.

Listening to Skip James singing 'Hard times here everywhere you go, Times is harder than ever been before,' or Son House shouting 'I wish I had me a heaven of my own, Well, I'd give all my women a long, long happy home,' or Bukka White chanting 'Believe I'm fixin' to die,' and all the misery and uncertainty and disappointment of existence is encapsulated in words that are often as incoherent and chaotic as life itself. The really great blues are honest and direct – they might use unfamiliar figures of speech, but in the work of a John Lee Hooker, Muddy Waters, or B. B. King, they speak to anyone who is willing to listen.

This is the reason why the blues has become the bedrock of western pop music: once you have heard Son House or Robert Johnson expressing their fears and emotions in music of savage exultation or barely expressible terror, everything else is just trimming and decoration. 'Got to keep moving,' sang Robert Johnson, 'Got to keep moving. Hellhound on my trail.' Is there anyone, anywhere, who can fail to understand such direct imagery and what it represents? Early blues writing often over-emphasized the romance of the blues, using beautiful phrases to hide the fact that not really a great deal was actually known about either the music or the musicians. That has changed, thanks to a small but dedicated bunch of researchers who have gone from door to door seeking out old 78s, tracked down many of the old singers themselves, and relentlessly pursued any clues to find out more about those mysterious and evocative names on records.

Of course, there is romance in the thought of a superb musician such as Jim Thompkins making just two recordings, one of which was never issued and whose presence in the scheme of things is noted and revered by a small handful of collectors on the strength of just one remarkable song. Who was he? Where did he come from? Was he really one-legged, as the Brunswick file entry for a Peg Leg Thompkins suggests? What was he doing in Memphis on February 21, 1930, and why did Brunswick only record two sides? Why is it that none of the Memphis musicians remember a man who was a powerful, vibrant singer, and a slide guitarist with a curious but compelling slack-string style? When his lone record was reissued on CD, it was included in an anthology called *Son House and the Great Delta Blues Singers*, which is pure guesswork. But what else can you do with a figure whose passage through life is marked by less than three minutes of music and an entry in a ledger?

Is there any wonder that so many listeners who are a generation and a world away from the source of all this magical music tend to get overwhelmed by the sheer romance of it all? How can a music that includes artists labelled as Peanut the Kidnapper, Black Spider Dumpling, Rabbit Brown, Hot Shot Willie, Sloppy Henry, Sweet Papa Tadpole and Kid Stormy Weather fail to stir the soul and whet the imagination? Why was Oscar Woods known as The Lone Wolf? Who gave Sam Hopkins the nickname Lightnin'? What possessed someone to call himself anything as unflattering as Leadbelly, Stickhorse, Iron Head, Muddy, Pig or Freezone? Could there really be singers called Arizona Dranes, Goldrush, Side Wheel Sally or Funny Paper, and was Bat the Hummingbird a person or a backwoods sport like Hunt the Possum? There were numerous Blind Willies, Lemons and Joes, as well as a Cripple Clarence, a couple of Peg Legs, a One Arm Slim (apparently a pianist!), a Sleepy John, a Babyface Thomas, a Bogus Blind Ben, and a number of Slims and Fats. What curious music was this, played by a bunch of individuals who sounded like a script from an hospital soap opera?

The songs were even more intriguing on paper. Who or what was the 'Molly Man' hymned by Moses Mason? Why did Smokey Harrison have the 'Iggly Oggly Blues', and were they painful? What had Jim Jackson been smoking if he 'Heard the Voice of a Pork Chop', and what on earth was the 'Bamalong' serenaded by Andrew and Jim Baxter?

And all those far-away places with strange sounding names – 'Rock Island Blues', 'Shelby County Workhouse Blues', 'Bunker Hill Blues', 'Brownsville Blues', 'Jonestown Blues' – and the obscure people given their moment of immortality on two and a half minutes of ancient wax – Tom Rushen, Aunt Caroline Dyer, Maggie Campbell, Lawyer Clark, Jim Canaan, Reachin' Pete. It was one great big, sprawling canvas, an epic novel in the making, with the characters all ready to go but with the background, the actions and the motivations yet to be fleshed out.

Of course the blues was romantic to Europeans – it was music about real people and real places, and you knew you could still wander down Beale Street, Third Street, 35th and Dearborn, and Madison Street if you knew where to look (and as long as unsentimental redevelopers hadn't got there first).

Did the earnest white copyists who jumped on the bright blue bandwagon in the sixties really appreciate what they were trying to steal when they imitated the dazzling Blind Blake rags, the frenetic hysteria of Robert Johnson preaching the blues, or the hypnotic, electric-slide riffs of Elmore James dusting his broom?

The old argument about whether white men can play the blues has long run its course – it really ended when Muddy Waters invited the white Charlie Musselwhite to join his band and the Bonzo Dog Doo Dah Band made fun of the whole debate with 'Can Blue Men Sing the Whites?' It doesn't really matter much anyway – if someone prefers to hear Jeremy Spencer of Fleetwood Mac playing Elmore James riffs instead of James himself, that's their privilege. All that matters is that listeners are aware that Spencer was a generation and several social strata away from the original, and that he was a disciple and not the guru. Those Blind Blake and Blind Boy Fuller rags are very much a part of every British guitarist's repertoire these days, and why not – they are good music which never had a problem in crossing racial barriers anyway.

The whole question of white blues singers must be defined, if at all, by tradition and culture, just as would happen if a white musician from a rural area attempted to play the generations-old music of those parts of Africa where music is almost a religion and played only by certain privileged families.

It is only in recent years, and largely thanks to a ground-breaking book by Tony Russell, that it has been slowly appreciated just how integrated music always was in rural communities, even those where the Ku Klux Klan ravaged and where racial barriers were absolute. The black musicians Andrew and Jim Baxter played with the white group The Georgia Yellowhammers; black slide guitarists Oscar Woods and Ed Shaffer accompanied white country singer (and later Governor of Louisiana) Jimmie Davis; blues yodeller Jimmy Rodgers recorded with both Louis Armstrong and bluesman Clifford Gibson, as well as rewriting a Clifford Hayes Jug Band number and recording it with the band. The black cajun accordionist Amèdè Ardoin had a white accompanist, fiddler Dennis McGee, and the duo, originally neighbouring sharecroppers, were a sensation. It didn't prevent white racists driving Ardoin into insanity and death, but it demonstrates how interwoven were the black and white musical traditions. 'Ebony and Ivory', as Stevie Wonder and Paul McCartney were later to sing.

★   ★   ★   ★

You could be forgiven for asking what exactly is the blues. The *Collins English Dictionary* defines it as 'a type of folk song originating among Black Americans at the beginning of the 20th century, usually employing a basic 12-bar chorus, the tonic, subdominant and dominant chords, frequent minor intervals and blue notes.' Blue notes? 'A flattened third of seventh, used frequently in the blues'.

All that means in simple English is that the blues generates a feeling of melancholy because it tends to concentrate on the notes in the cracks of the Western scales – as does much of the African music that is one of the building blocks of the blues – and also the minor chords that are used so effectively to create a feeling of pessimism and tension by many great classical composers, particularly the English Ralph Vaughan Williams whose music was steeped in the folk music of his own country.

Musicological analysis is for the scholars and the theorists, and should never be allowed to be a barrier to simply enjoying the music. It doesn't matter if we know little about the men and women who actually made the recordings – although certainly some knowledge of who and what they were helps to set the music in context. But in the same way that Jewish opera fans can appreciate Wagner's music without approving of Wagner's anti-Semitism, or condemning him because Hitler loved his music, so too can we enjoy the many different strands of the blues without condoning, or even knowing about, the social conditions that gave it birth. No knowledge is wasted, and appreciation of the blues is increased and deepened by even a surface understanding of the background. It does help, too, in trying to understand what blues actually is.

Unfortunately, the 'blues' tag was added to all kinds of dreary pop songs in the twenties, and many so-called blues are little more than Tin Pan Alley garbage dressed up to look more important than they really are. Many of what are known as classic blues singers – usually, female stage and cabaret performers – were a long way from any kind of folk music, and there is little merit – apart from occasionally some spectacular jazz accompaniments – in stuff like 'Mama Whip',

The grim reality of life for America's black citizens in the heartland of the blues. Draughty wooden shacks, often with simple tar-paper roofs and few facilities, were home to large families who had little chance of bettering their conditions in the Deep South. Countless blues singers grew up in homes such as these in Yazoo City, Mississippi, the kind of places serenaded bitterly by Texan Mercy Dee Walton in 'One Room Country Shack' and 'Log Cabin Blues'.

PHOTOGRAPH: SYLVIA PITCHER

'Mama Spank If Her Daddy Don't Come Home', or 'You Better Keep the Home Fires Burning ('cause Your Mama's Getting Cold)'. It took someone extra special, like the majestic Bessie Smith, to transcend the banality of mild smut such as 'Kitchen Man' or 'Put It Right Here'. The way that such a perceptive, sensitive artist can change such second-rate dross into a beautifully structured, perfectly sung performance is a mark of why such superlative blues singers are equal in artistry to any opera singer or other kind of folk musician. And it wasn't just the more sophisticated artists who had the magic touch with material scarcely worth their talents. Charley Patton may make a total hash of trying to sing 'Running Wild', but hear how that magic transmutation works on equally limited material, such as 'Shake it and Break It'.

But the key to the blues doesn't lie in the endless cabaret blues of the twenties, or the smart cocktail singers of later years. Compare Ray Charles' earlier records in the forties, when he was trying to be a smarmy, Nat King Cole/Charles Brown-style crooner, with his Atlantic sides of the fifties, when he allowed his feeling for the blues and gospel to surface, and an understanding producer encouraged him to create some of the most exciting and innovative rhythm and blues ever recorded. Charles is no more a straight blues singer than Fats Domino or Bo Diddley, but the blues lies at the core of all their music, and would be nothing without that underlying vitality.

In 1964, R. M. W. Dixon and J. Godrich published a discography listing every known blues and gospel record made until 1943. A fourth edition is imminent, for it is considerably out of date, thanks to the tireless research of dedicated collectors. Naturally, the pair needed to define the blues and, equally naturally, not everyone agrees with their definition.

'We have tried to evolve some more or less consistent criterion for inclusion… based mainly on the prevailing opinions among folk-musicologists and collectors as to what is genuinely "black" – that is, performed in a style peculiar to black performances and not derivative or a copy of any white style… The dividing line has been hard to draw and around this line, decisions have had to be somewhat arbitrary,' they wrote. 'The reader can assume that unless an artist is listed here, he is almost certainly not a blues artist.'

No one could criticize such an incomparable labour of love which has become the bible of blues collectors, but there is no doubt that the greater availability of obscure blues 78s has made that definition seem more arbitrary than it at first seemed.

Jazz singers as such are said to be not included, yet there is little of that elusive 'black' quality in the remorseless pages of classic 'blues' by people such as the amiable Eva Taylor, whose work is really collected for her superlative accompanists, and not for her racially indeterminate voice. Someone like Lulu Jackson offered little or no blues element in simple country ballads such as 'You're Going to Leave the Old Home Jim', yet she is included, while the beautiful, moving, piano blues and solos recorded by Jelly Roll Morton for the Library of Congress – music as 'black' and bluesy as anyone could wish – don't make it, presumably because Morton is best known as a jazz musician. Some jug bands, such as the Phillips Louisville Jug Band, are included, while others that are closely allied and with a very similar approached are exiled.

In retrospect, Godrich and Dixon erred with considerable caution in some directions, and spread their net too wide in others. Again, it should be emphasized that no criticism is intended or implied – the point is made simply to underline just how difficult it is to define the blues and how the word means different things to different people. Elvis Presley sang blues, so did Eddie Cochran and Jerry Lee Lewis, but it was called rock 'n' roll or rockabilly, in order to make it socially acceptable to white southerners. Eric Clapton and John Mayall are often closer to what is usually accepted as the traditional form of blues than is Robert Cray, or any of the other, younger, black singers whose music leans more to soul and rhythm and blues than to 12-bar.

The first tentative post-war blues discography omitted most of Leadbelly's recordings, on the dubious ground that they were folk music rather than blues, and left out many respected artists on the equally fraught reasoning that they leaned too far towards rock. If defining pre-war blues is difficult, trying to set boundaries on the post-war music is virtually impossible, and a revised version of the post-war book has acknowledged the problem by including recordings which barely qualify under any reasonable criteria. But that's better than imposing personal taste or foolishly attempting to define the indefinable.

It is still difficult to tell if some records are by black or white bands – The Two Poor Boys, the Mississippi Mud Steppers, the Mississippi Sheiks, Hayes and Prater, the Old Pal Smoke Shop Four and the Kansas City Blues Strummers were all black (or thought to be), while Taylor's Kentucky Boys were mixed race – and no one really knows about The Too Bad Boys, who were possibly the white Westbrook Conservatory Entertainers in down-home disguise, or the curious Cedar Creek Sheik. Harmonica Frank, the white, post-war entertainer who sang blues, was long thought to be black, as was the maniacal Monroe Moe Jackson, while a question mark still hangs over Julius King, Rhythm Willie, and several others. These are not names from the distant past, but evidence of a continuing shared tradition in rural America.

Black musicians played for white functions, white musicians learned from black. A. P. and Maybelle Carter, of the white country group The Carter Family, picked up much of their style and repertoire from black guitarist Leslie Riddle, who was apparently a frequent guest at the Carter home, and it was Riddle, who was himself unrecorded, who may have taught Maybelle the steel guitar figures she uses on the Carters' huge hit, 'Little Pal of Mine'.

Jimmie Rodgers yodels permeate the blues of the thirties: the sound of black America in turn pervades much of the white country music, particularly that of Rogers himself. Frank Hutchinson from West Virginia learned from two itinerant black musicians and played stunning slide guitar in the authentic black style on his 32 records. Blind Riley Puckett from Georgia recorded with the Skillet Lickers, but also made a handful of solos, including 'A Darkey's Wail', which he learned from a black musician on Atlanta's Decatur Street. The romantic view is that the musician may have been Willie McTell, and certainly the dates and the style fit, so why not? Bawdy white musician Cliff Carlisle's style owes much to Curley Weaver and Buddy Moss, while the sides that black guitarist Oscar Woods made with Kitty Gray's band show the influence of white Western Swing, which itself combined country music and blues with big band swing.

The examples are endless, but the conclusion is the same – music was music, and if a white musician liked a black sound, or vice versa, then there was no social disgrace in adapting it. There's an old rumour that the very primitive sounding, black harmonica player Jaybird Coleman was actually managed by his local Ku Klux Klan. Like the apocryphal tale of McTell and Puckett, if it isn't true, it really ought to be.

So blues was always a multi-racial music. More important, surely, is the fact that it was the one musical common denominator for the poor, the exploited, the wage slaves of both races who often shared the same deprivations in the mines, the factories and the fields. It was a music that grew from and within those mixed communities, and who can say where the black or the white influence began and ended? Listen to Cannon's Jug Stompers on 'Featherbed Blues' (which may predate the Civil War) and discover the same song recorded by old-time veteran Uncle Dave

Macon as 'Over the Road I'm Bound to Go'. Turn to the gospel and blues singer Blind Joe Taggart for two tracks that respected blues writer Ken Romanowski contends offer a time trip into the period in the south after the Civil War when a joint black and white musical tradition existed. Everyone knows the fervent gospel of the sanctified black groups like McIntorsh and Edwards, Elder Richard Bryant and others: yet just as frenetic and free-form are white hot gospelers, like the great Ernest Phipps and his congregation.

Shared communities, shared problems, shared traditions. So the whole argument about whether white men can sing the blues is over before it starts. There are few white singers with the fervent passion of a Son House or Charley Patton, or the delicacy of a Willie McTell, but the further back in time you go – at least to the Civil War – the more difficult it is to state absolutely the origins of a song or style. There are echoes of flamenco in some blues (Buddy Boy Hawkins) which presumably came home with the soldiers from the First World War. The slide guitar is probably Hawaiian, or perhaps an attempt to imitate the fiddle (an Afro-American favourite earlier than the guitar), although a fairly natural development once you have a string that needs modulating in some way. But when even a foundation-stone bluesman like Skip James can record a country song ('Drunken Spree') and the much-worshiped Charley Patton can turn in an incoherent adaptation of the pop song 'Running Wild', it comes as no surprise that the mighty Robert Johnson used to perform 'My Blue Heaven' and 'Yes Sir, That's My Baby'.

And just think of the incredible journey of the bawdy medieval ballad 'Our Gudeman', which resurfaced this century as 'Seven Drunken Nights' by Irish group The Dubliners, and 'Wake Up Old Lady' by Sonny Boy Williamson in Chicago. Now *that* is integration. There are other examples. Generations of English peasants who had never even seen a black man would recognize 'Derbytown' by Old Ced Odom and Diamond Lil Hardaway, while Blind Blake – or someone using his name – recorded a music-hall song called 'Champagne Charlie is my Name', which celebrates Charles Heideseck, founder of the champagne house of that name. Did Blake ever taste champagne, or was he even vaguely aware of Champagne Charlie as a real person? It is vital to remember that recordings merely scratch the surface of the average so-called blues singers' repertoire, and the distorted picture they present does a considerable disservice to history. Luckily, artists such as Leadbelly, Willie McTell, Mance Lipscomb, John Jackson and a few others had the opportunity to redress that imbalance, and their recordings take them far beyond the blues, or even white country music.

Black and white country music did drift apart over the years, although the links were always there, and becoming stronger in jazz. Rock 'n' roll, that glorious, great, musical stewpot, turned everything upside down again as white musicians such as Elvis Presley took the black music of the communities in which they grew up, and sanitized it for white audiences. Listen to Elvis singing songs by Junior Parker, Big Boy Crudup and Smiley Lewis, and there is no sense of a white boy copying the blacks.

Presley, and a few others like him, were singing the music with which they grew up, and that's the difference between them and the later white blues revivalists, who simply imitated what they had heard on record with no experience of the background, the whys and the wherefores of what made the music the way it is. A young British white blues player is so far removed from the original it is difficult to understand what credibility can be expected or achieved. The same problem faces British musicians who dress up in cowboy hats and check shirts and moon plaintively about truck drivers, bar-room queens and the whole mid-West redneck culture, or the English cajun bands. If white blues singers are divorced from the original by race, colour and culture, the cajun copyists are trying to lay claim to a music that is a unique amalgam of French language and a veritable maelstrom of music from all over the world, magically transformed into something uniquely American. It would be more acceptable if all these yearners after the American dream were reviving something dead and forgotten, like the Cornish language, but the original music, and many genuinely original performers, are still alive and active.

On the other hand, there are those who take from the blues and build upon the foundation without knocking down the walls merely to see how they are put together. Eric Clapton, who knows the music intimately, has never seemed a bleak copyist. Ralph McTell's reworkings of Blind Blake's rags are always worth hearing, and the way that Rory McLeod has adapted Sonny Terry's falsetto and harmonica playing for his own polemic rants is impressive. Other performers blend a touch of blues, a hint of cajun and a flash of Africa or India in a pleasing, and often highly creative, musical gumbo.

Sir Michael Tippett, a very uncompromising British classical composer, included a blues in his Third Symphony, and American William Russo has written several pieces for orchestra and blues band that are very successful. And there are always exceptions, like Jo-Ann Kelly, a British blues singer who always gave the impression of really feeling and experiencing the whole essence of the blues, or Ottilie Patterson, a superlative blues shouter whose finest moments bear comparison with Bessie Smith. Once again, there is no sense of blatant plagiarism in either. They take the originals and add something of themselves, and if they are neither black nor American, nor raised in the places or conditions that gave rise to the blues, then they overcome such disadvantages by acknowledging a debt, and borrowing rather than stealing.

Frank Scott, a Briton now running America's biggest specialist record distributor in California, provided a very perceptive review of a collection of British blues in his 1991 *The Downhome Guide to the Blues*. He praised the performers for trying to remain faithful to the spirit of the old black guitarists, but he was scathing about the vocals, variously described as unconvincing or very silly, apart from Jo-Ann Kelly's convincing performance of a Memphis Minnie song. 'There is nothing here for the serious blues enthusiast,' concluded Scott, 'but it certainly is fun.' That sums it all up pretty well — certainly considerably better than the anonymous person who told the wide-ranging and adventurous European magazine *Blueprint*: 'In the beginning, *Blueprint* was a good idea, but now all it supports is old black blokes.'

Blueprint let him off lightly, apart from a dig at his 'inherent racism', but, in the same article, defined a view of the blues which obviously appeals to a considerable number of listeners. It's well worth quoting in full for its thoughtful championship of the blues as a music which has now transcended its origins.

'From the beginning we have considered and promoted the blues in its widest possible sense. Although we will always take cognizance of the fact that the music emerged as an Afro-American style in a specific cultural context, we also acknowledge that this context has diversified, along with the ethnic make-up of the performers.'

After pointing out that modern blues incorporates overtones of jazz, rock, soul, rap, and even World Music, the magazine continues: 'For us the blues is an evolving, contemporary musical form and not a museum piece or collector's item. Nor, we believe, should any arbitrary parameters be placed on the music's continuing development. For these reasons we have consistently tried to cover all shades of blue — artists both black and white, American or British/European, acoustic or

There's a grim irony in the fact that the name of white plantation owner Will Dockery is known worldwide today because of one black musician who worked on his Mississippi farm – Charley Patton. Will Dockery, son of a Confederate Colonel who lost his fortune in the Civil War, had 10,000 acres of former swamp in Sunflower County and called himself a merchant and farmer. A Mississippi newspaper described him as the Delta's greatest philanthropist. Pictured here is the entrance to Dockery's plantation.

PHOTOGRAPH: SYLVIA PITCHER

electric, male or female, those working within a traditional definition of the blues or those who refused to be bound by stylistic limitations.'

That is honest, liberal and generous, from a British magazine that sells in Europe and America, and probably a more popular view – in Europe at least – than any doomed attempt to see the blues as a black American art form.

When the white guitarist Ry Cooder, an enthusiast for all kinds of authentic American music, plays with a traditional Indian or African musician, what level of authenticity does that create – especially when said musician has plugged in an electric guitar – and does it matter? We all live in one world these days and while music never had boundaries, the definitions are blurring.

White guitarist John Fahey, who helped rediscover Bukka White, blends the sounds of Deep South blues and many other kinds of American music into seamless tone poems that, at one minute, can hint at Charley Patton doodling on a hot summer day by the Mississippi, at another the elegance of medieval Spain, at a third a country hoedown or a jazz band on a riverboat. Like Cooder and the technically gifted Leo Kottke, Fahey captures the essence of black American music and transmutes it into the kind of cultural stew that Cooder, in particular, relishes. Wisely, Fahey doesn't sing – playing like a black guitarist is one thing, trying to sing like one is invariably embarrassing.

Irish musicians play Bulgarian music, the classically trained Kronos String Quartet dabbles in folk music from around the globe as well as Monk and Ellington, the music of African pygmies and Australian aborigines is blended into western rhythms and reaches the pop charts. Purism in any music, let alone the blues, is becoming the sign of a closed mind and a fettered imagination. Thanks to records, nearly a century of black American music can be savoured in its original purity (forgetting, of course, the input of record executives who ordered only what they wanted to hear). Perhaps now is the time to follow the *Blueprint* path and accept the blues as just one strand in a wholly remarkable slow fusion of national musics from across the globe.

A few last thoughts on this whole question of whether the blues is an indigenous folk music, or simply another kind of note bashing that can be just as authentically performed by whites as blacks. Bob Brunning, a founder member of Fleetwood Mac, among others, and a strong advocate for British blues, claimed in his book *The Blues in Britain* (updated edition, Blandford, 1995): 'There is no simple answer, even if the question itself is suspectly racist.' That is politically correct nonsense. Apparently, even questioning the validity of a movement which relies largely upon imitating the art of another race and another nation is now racist.

Brunning also claims that British R&B bands are helping to keep the music 'as a live entity rather than a sterile academic branch of American culture'. One look at the hundreds of contemporary blues CDs in the catalogue of British mail-order specialists *Red Lick* will demonstrate what a curiously narrow and inaccurate vision that is. There have never been so many blues records of so many kinds easily available for all to enjoy, and surely true sterility lies more in regarding artless imitation as creativity. Brunning also fails to see any difference between authentic singers and authentic *sounding* singers, such as Joe Cocker, Jo-Ann Kelly and others. Imagine the reaction if one applied the same careless judgement to an English writer who wrote *like* William Faulkner or Norman Mailer, or a British painter who turned out canvases *like* Jackson Pollock or Andy Warhol? Brunning himself might recreate the sound of Chicago blues in full flight with his De Luxe Blues Band, but it could be argued that his main career as a London head teacher is a dubious qualification to empathize with the cultural background underlying a predominantly black, working class, American music.

But Brunning is absolutely right when he says that it was the young British bands that inspired many Americans, black and white, to rediscover their black musical culture – indeed, it was the Rolling Stones who led me and countless others, via Chuck Berry and Bo Diddley, into the marvellous, unsuspected world of the real blues. He is also right when he says than most American bluesmen couldn't care less about whether accompanists are black or white, so long as they have a feel for the music – but does that negate the argument? There might be a touch of diplomacy in John Lee Hooker's fulsome praise of the British Groundhogs after a tour with them in the sixties, or Robert Cray's oft-quoted: 'Anyone can play the blues. They don't have to be black', but it was Hooker who also said during the British blues boom: 'People have been listening to the blues for years. Now they're playing it outside the States, and it's breaking out everywhere, spreading like a cancer.' Your reading of that will depend on which side you take in the argument, but cancers don't tend to be beneficial. The setting in which the blues were born still exists in rural Mississippi, probably the poorest area of America and the one with the highest number of unemployed and illiterate people. And the blues is still played in the old way in juke joints and bars in every Delta town. A company in Memphis called Mississippi Resources offers a two-day blues trip, which is probably the best way for those who can't face a still-threatening environment on their own. You can visit Robert Johnson's burial site – two of them, in fact, depending on which story you believe – or the old log cabin on Stovall's Plantation where Muddy Waters once lived. There is Junior Kimbrough's juke joint in nearby Holly Springs, or Smitty's Red Top bar in Clarksdale, blues capital of the Delta and one-time home of Patton, House, Johnson, Muddy, Elmore James and many, many more.

Few tourists ever venture into backwoods Mississippi, but those that do usually go for the blues and places celebrated in the music, such as Friars Point, Highway 61, Vicksburg, Belzoni and Greenville. Up north, there are even tours of the remains of old Harlem, dangerous home of urban blues, soul and jazz for nearly a century. Perhaps there is a dusty flavour of the museum about it all and, as I found in Atlanta, young blacks do prefer rap and other modern sounds to what they regard as Uncle Tom music, but the music still lives where it was born – in the heart of communities where people still make their own music.

It is difficult to really appreciate just how very foreign the ill-educated, hard-living blues singers who travelled the south were to the average European listener. It is easy to respond to a city slicker like Muddy Waters in his snappy suits, or Sonny Boy Williamson in his bizarre Pied Piper outfit. They were streetwise, and knew their place in the scheme of things, and had grown away from country ways.

Muddy was delighted when the Rolling Stones called themselves after one of his records and were willing to acknowledge him as the master. Sonny Boy was known to turn on hapless European accompanists and order them to shut up before continuing a set on his own. Like Skip James, he remained aloof and enigmatic.

With Sonny Boy, Son House, Bukka White and Skip James, finding a common meeting place in the short time allowed was impossible. I remember Son, laboriously signing programmes backstage after a concert and impassively greeting and politely thanking the young white kids whose lives and upbringing were so far removed that they might have come from different planets. How could anyone bridge the gap between a tumbledown, backwoods bar in deepest Mississippi where Son was among his own people, and this smart concert hall several thousand miles away? Bukka White was more outgoing, willing to exchange pleasantries, but still withdrawn and suspicious as any man would be with his experience of the white race. House, White and Skip James had all been involved with violent death in their past. Where was the key, the link to the inner person, between a white kid from a prosperous background and these men, one of whom had served time in America's most famous and feared prison, Parchman Farm? It's better never to link the artist and the art. It's a bad mistake to meet one's heroes – their creations should speak for them, and the person behind that creation should remain private.

We would lose so much great music, art and acting if we had to approve of the way that the practitioners behaved at those times when they belong solely to themselves, and not to us. Muddy Waters was polite when I asked him at a club date if he would play bottleneck guitar as he used to. He'd heard that one before, accepted the interest and the naivety of the question – and declined. He didn't do bottleneck any more, it was too country, and this was the tough, city, Muddy band with a white harmonica player. Bottleneck was the past: the fact that a white player was willing to play subordinate to a black musician was the future. Who can blame Muddy for refusing to accept those who insisted his best work was in the late forties and early fifties and that he had been in decline ever since. In retrospect, perhaps, the critics were right and Muddy wrong, but at the time, he was alive and performing, and not ready to be classified into early, middle and late periods. This was Now.

But blues singers are like other heroes – it's best to cherish their art without seeking to dig too deeply into their souls. Their music lodges in the memory through its beauty, its timeless power to move, its resonance, and the way it summons up other worlds and other truths. It also reminds listeners that, as so many musicians are demonstrating these days, we are indeed one world, for the blues speaks to anyone who listens more directly and frankly than almost any other folk music. The fact that Son House was reserved, Bukka White was wary, and Skip James and Sonny Boy simply unwilling to communicate, does nothing to diminish the power of their true and (for us) their only legacy – the music.

Then there was Fred McDowell – Mississippi Fred. Fred was different. He had been discovered by Alan Lomax on one of his field recording trips in the southern states, and was a remarkable find. He had been around in the twenties, playing for local dances, picnics and parties in Tennessee and across the Mississippi Delta. Dwell for a moment on that magic word – Mississippi. So much more is known about the blues these days, and Mississippi blues can now be seen as just one root of a gigantic, sprawling vine; but for many collectors, the records and artists from the state which once stood for everything cruel and inhumane in the relationship between black and white remain the rawest, the most appealing, and the most durable.

Charley Patton, the incoherent sound of musical chaos barely restrained by normal notes and harmonies, left his mark on Mississippi, although few dared walk in his footprints. His music was rough and sometimes undisciplined, his voice forced and hard to understand, his guitar work heavy, occasionally repetitive, but also stunningly effective. There are few moments more enduring in the blues than Patton at his best: on the dancing 'Mississippi Bo Weavil Blues', where his eloquent slide guitar becomes a second voice; on 'Hammer Blues', with its melodic whines against an insistent bass line; in the churning duets with Willie Brown, like 'Moon Going Down'; and, most of all, the astonishing passion and breathtaking rhythmic drive of 'High Water Everywhere'. This is poorly recorded music, but more than any in this field, it transcends technical limitations. It is difficult to think of any real Patton disciples, although there are hints of his approach in some of Bukka White's vocals, and certainly in the way that Howlin' Wolf sang in the early days, albeit with an urban overlay. That could be because Patton did things his way, and it was easier for others to follow Son House or Tommy Johnson.

Son House, greatest of the handful of Mississippi originals who lived long enough to play for collectors rather than for his own people, worked and recorded with Patton, and at times his guitar playing, with its descriptive bottleneck embellishments, becomes even closer to free form than does Patton's. His masterpiece is the two-part 'Preaching the Blues', a declamatory piece which House later admitted represented his indecision over whether to be a blues singer or gospel preacher (then two very different worlds, as shown by the way blues singers usually adopted pseudonyms for when they recorded their religious numbers). Yet it is hardly complimentary about the church, with lines such as 'I'm gonna be a Baptist preacher and I sure won't have to work', and few church-goers would have appreciated his wish to have a Heaven of his own so that he could 'give all my women a long, long happy home'. The song also includes one of the most famous verses of all, one which turned up so often elsewhere it is probably part of the large bank of floating images used by every singer. 'I met the blues this morning, walking just like a man. I said "Good morning blues, now gimme your right hand." ' Simple, direct, poetic, and eminently appealing in its image of the blues as a kind of nature spirit who can be supplicated, rejected, or welcomed.

This sophisticated bunch of well-dressed club-goers include three of the biggest names in thirties' blues. Enjoying a social night out are the great Texas pianist Big Maceo Merriweather (left), the ubiquitous Big Bill Broonzy (third from left) and big-selling rhythm and blues vocalist Lil Green (fourth from left). Rose Broonzy is between Big Maceo and her husband, and the three on the right are Jimmy (a friend), Mrs Lucille Merriweather, and Little T (Tyrell Dixon), Maceo's drummer.

PHOTOGRAPH: COURTESY MIKE ROWE

Son recorded just a handful of songs in 1930, but they remain among the most powerful and influential of all. Even Patton never quite reached the level of emotion of House at his most fervent, when the fury of his inner vision drove the music almost to the point of rhythmic breakdown. Eleven years later, that intensity had diminished somewhat when he was recorded at length and with a small group for the Library of Congress, but the tension he builds up on the long 'Government Fleet Blues', with Willie Brown's bass pounding away behind slide guitar work that is impassioned even by House's standards, is quite incomparable.

Interestingly, many of the songs that Son recorded in 1941 and 1942 derive from Patton's repertoire, yet it was House, not Patton, who overshadowed those younger players, such as Robert Johnson and Muddy Waters, who went on to lay the foundations for rock 'n' roll and soul. He also recorded a peculiarly structured, country pop song about the Second World War, and a version of Blind Lemon Jefferson's 'See That My Grave is Kept Clean'. These underline both Jefferson's widespread popularity and that oft-repeated point about commercial records being unrepresentative of the average singer's full repertoire. The Library of Congress recordings also captured the sound of a steam train on a branch line behind the store where the recording was taking place, an accident of timing that created one of the most eerily romantic moments in the history of recorded blues.

But there were others around in Mississippi in Fred McDowell's early days, apart from Patton and House. Skip James was a true giant, a solitary, brooding character who admitted killing several men and was, by all accounts, a loner all his life. But the 18 tracks he recorded with his own guitar and piano in 1931 stand firm as the most remarkable legacy of the blues. Some were simple spirituals, the rest a bizarre range of unremittingly gloomy blues in a startling variety of styles.

His biographer, Stephen Calt, believes James had no concept of the blues as entertainment. His aim was to impress with his technical skills and to manipulate the emotions — to deaden the minds of his listeners, as he rather startlingly phrased it. It's hard to think of a better way of summing up the frisson, the unique sense of blackness that James' music instils in the listener. The nearest he got to simple entertainment was probably 'Drunken Spree', a hillbilly square dance usually known as 'It Was Late Last Night When My Johnny [or Billy] Came Home', but even there, his uncompromising flat vocal added the menace found in all his music. Better, far better, was the breakneck guitar accompaniment to the spiritual 'I'm So Glad', which Eric Clapton and Cream revived in the sixties; or his frenzied and startling piano pyrotechnics on '22-20 Blues' and 'If You Haven't Any Hay' – unparalleled sides which hint at anger and lurking madness.

These extraordinary displays of fiery temperament contrast with the cold, austere face that James presents in his other blues, which are full of depressing images of cypress-shadowed graveyards and chilly, unfulfilling personal relationships. Little of his music fits any kind of formula, especially the piano sides. Even when he is apparently responding to outside inspiration, such as his version of Leroy Carr's 'How Long', which approaches contemptuous parody, or '22-20', a spontaneous reaction to Roosevelt Sykes' '44 Blues', the relationship to the originals ranges from sparse to non-existent. Perhaps even more astonishing, James' guitar and piano playing were completely dissimilar, unlike most other multi-instrumentalists, who tended to echo the sound and approach of one instrument when switching to another.

Neither does James fit easily into any group of musicians, although others playing in a similarly eccentric style have been recorded in recent years in his home town of Bentonia. If the blues can really be said to have a genius, then Skip James is the sinister contender for the title.

The difference between James and Patton, and Patton and Tommy Johnson, is so wide at times that it is difficult so understand how Mississippi blues was ever regarded as one style. That is very unfair, however – it wasn't until the reissue labels began making rare 78s (many with just one battered copy surviving) available to all that any informed understanding was possible. Even in the last decade, there have been remarkable discoveries, such as never-before-heard test pressings by House, Patton and Johnson, and the unearthing of lone copies of long-lost 78s. That romantic theme again – the awe at hearing music only a handful have experienced in the past half century that can affect the most seasoned collectors.

But Tommy Johnson, and his colleague Ishman Bracey, were far removed from the hoarse, passion-driven, preaching style of Patton and House. Johnson was an alcoholic with a light, colourful voice which generated a yearning wistfulness. He recorded a small handful of sides for the Victor company in 1928 which remain, like James' brief recording session, as memorable as anything ever waxed from Mississippi. 'Cool Drink of Water Blues', 'Maggie Campbell', 'Canned Heat Blues', 'Bye Bye Blues' – each a sensitive, polished gem with a delicacy and sophistication not usually associated with Mississippi. The whole package is given even greater strength by the guitar of Charlie McCoy, a seminal and under-appreciated player, which interweaves with Johnson's to suggest a much bigger unit at work. This is music that reverberates down the years.

The same effect is found in the duets of Frank Stokes and Dan Sane, Joe Callicott and Garfield Akers, Memphis Minnie and Joe McCoy, or the Huff Brothers, who were still playing the old style in the fifties. It is, as British writer Paul Oliver put it, the Mississippi blues at its most expressive and poetic.

Undiluted, quality country blues were still being recorded commercially in Mississippi in the fifties and well into the sixties by collectors visiting rural communities with tape recorders. And that is where Fred McDowell surfaces. He could have been another Kid Bailey or Willie Brown if the breaks had gone his way. He might have appeared on one of those picturesque Paramount 78s, with their eagle labels, their fried-egg surfaces and primitive recording techniques, but the right people didn't notice him. Part of this romance of the blues is the sheer haphazard nature of it all.

The white talent scouts who served the blues labels knew their business and managed to get many major talents recorded. But names revered today didn't always sell and record companies were, naturally enough, commercial concerns. They wanted artists who would appeal to buyers and some, like the highly regarded Buddy Boy Hawkins and Bo Weavil Jackson, didn't.

Some time ago there was a rapidly discredited theory that all the worthwhile blues singers had been recorded – which patently isn't so. Stories of unheard giants who were invariably better than anyone who actually recorded loom large in the recollections of musicians, and, even after accepting the natural urge to exaggerate, there is no doubt whatsoever that those who did record were merely a representative sample. Fred McDowell was one of those who didn't; so was Eli Green, a pupil of Charley Patton who finally made a couple of pure Delta blues records for Chris Strachwitz of Arhoolie with Fred accompanying. In his youth, Eli must have been magnificent. But Fred was younger, and although he saw Patton perform and knew records by Blind Lemon Jefferson, he remained a community musician until 1960, when Alan Lomax heard about this remarkable singer-guitarist living near Como, Mississippi.

Fred was then in his fifties, and in his prime. Lomax recorded him after dark at his farm, with one microphone for his voice, one for his guitar and one for his aunt, Fannie Evans, who accompanied him on some tracks with surprisingly effective comb and paper. In his eloquent book, *The Land Where the Blues Began*, Lomax recalled poetically how Fred sounded like a deep-voiced black herald, with a silver voiced heavenly choir answering him back from the treble strings. He loved recording and felt his fortune had been made. Perhaps it had, in a small way, but at least Fred was widely recorded in the following years, travelled far and received some financial and emotional return from the many years of honing and perfecting his prodigious talent.

Considering that such a major musician had to wait until 1960 to be discovered begs the question once more about how many other first-class bluesmen lived and died in obscurity, with not even one of those elusive 78s to their name. It's not worth pursuing the point too far, because there is no way of ever knowing. But the fact that Fred, and a previously unknown, devastating bottleneck player called John Dudley, could be found still active at a time when rock 'n' roll was already ruling the music world says much for the durability and lasting appeal of the country blues.

When Fred surfaced, no one was aware that Son House, Bukka White, Skip James, Ishman Bracey, Mississippi John Hurt, Sleepy John Estes, John Henry Barbee and many other pre-war recording artists were still alive, yet here was a total unknown playing in that true, surging, Delta style, and with a power and impact of which Patton or House would have been proud.

Fred was a superb singer, in the hoarse, declamatory style of the great Mississippi shouters, but his slide-guitar playing – he used a piece of bottleneck less than an inch wide – was superlative. His repertoire was a mixture of traditional material he had heard on records or radio, or picked up during his years of wandering, but he had a real gift as an improviser, reworking and reshaping familiar material in a way that was uniquely his own. Listen to any of his recordings of the Mississippi standard 'Shake 'em On Down' to hear how far he takes it from versions by Big Joe Williams or Bukka White.

Fred's best recordings are probably those from a long, informal session he did for collector Dick Spottswood in 1962, which curiously remained unissued for more than 20 years. Many of the songs are not recorded elsewhere; some are the first versions of themes he reused endlessly on his many albums. But it is the evocative atmosphere of the recording session which makes these sides so beautiful and special. Fred is relaxed and in superb form, and he plays and sings against a

background of children playing and neighbours chattering and enjoying their man's moment of fame. Nothing else he did has this sense of community, of music that is part of everyday life and springing directly from it, rather than being recreated in a studio.

In 1969, he toured Europe, and one of his dates was a blues club in Bristol run by Ian A. Anderson, a white country blues singer, one of the earliest experimenters in mixing musical traditions, and now editor of the seminal and eclectic British magazine *Folk Roots*. Most of the guests were British, of course – people like Alexis Korner, who once let me reverently touch the one known copy of Skip James' 'I'm so Glad', and the late, lamented Jo-Ann Kelly and her brother Dave, who is now part of The Blues Band. Occasionally there were real black American blues singers, like pianist Curtis Jones, a quiet, polite man who, in retrospect, was as unmemorable as his many records. And Fred, who could never be unmemorable.

It's a long time ago, but I remember watching open-mouthed at the way a touch from his little glass slide could produce such a devastatingly *big* sound. It was all there – the

The car plants of Detroit were a magnet for black families heading north to seek a better life, and the city became a major post-war blues centre. John Lee Hooker, Eddie Burns, 'Baby Boy' Warren, Bobo Jenkins and others cut their musical teeth in clubs like the Harlem Inn – pictured here in 1948, its name reflecting the venerable jazz and blues tradition of the famous New York district before Detroit acquired a real identity of its own.

PHOTOGRAPH: COURTESY BOBO JENKINS

compulsive Mississippi rhythms, the shouted vocals, the way the slide would make the guitar talk as it slid down the frets. Even Son House, just two years his senior, didn't have Fred's involvement and presence – although, to be fair, Fred had been playing regularly, while House had been brought out of musical retirement.

Afterwards we took him to an Indian restaurant. It was the time of civil-rights marches and general racial unrest in America, and Fred had spent most of his life in backwoods Mississippi. He was clearly uneasy about sitting in a public restaurant with a bunch of white youngsters – Alan Lomax's *The Land where the Blues Began* offers graphic evidence of how the police in the southern states regarded mixed-race socializing. But no thug in a white hood appeared and the local policeman didn't even give him a second glance, and he gradually relaxed. It wasn't an easy evening – his thick southern accent and that completely different cultural background were obstacles, and Lord knows what he made of the mysteries of an Indian menu. But it was a good few hours and I'd like to think we put him at his ease as much as we could and that he had warm memories to take back to Como.

Surprisingly for such an archaic (for the sixties) performer, Fred was never stuck in a time warp. It didn't take long for the dungarees to disappear and a gold-and-silver, Elvis-style suit and electric guitar to appear. Fred took to the late 20th century with enthusiasm, and while he always insisted: 'I play the country blues in the old style, none of that rock 'n' roll, y' understand', his music remained at least half a century behind his ostentatious outfits. Electric guitars simply amplified what he had been doing so perfectly for years. They gave an added edge (or reduced the subtlety, depending on your viewpoint) and allowed him to develop the techniques he had already pushed to the limits on acoustic instruments. His very percussive style needed electricity less than most, and he did let the mechanics override the inspiration in later years, but if he wanted to be an electric bluesman and refused to be preserved in aspic, who can blame him?

Fred died of cancer in 1972, after 10 good years as the darling of the white blues fans. He doesn't seem to have been cheated or sold down the river like so many others, and he always appeared to be genuinely delighted at being able to share his music with so many people around the world. Christ Strachwitz, whose Arhoolie label gave Fred his first LP, wrote his obituary in a few, deeply-felt lines in a CD reissue of that early work: 'Fred McDowell was a wonderful person and one of the most sensitive artists I have ever heard. His dedication to his music was total and he never thought twice about sharing it with anyone who came to hear it or enjoyed it livening up a dance party.'

Could anyone want to leave this life with a better memorial than that?

The blues, of course, is much more than the Mississippi music of 70 years ago. It is a living, vibrant statement that has gone though many changes to reflect the swings in musical taste, and much of what is called blues today would be only just about recognizable to those who recorded for Paramount, Victor, Vocalion and ARC all those years ago.

Some of those early musicians would be able to adapt with ease and pleasure, as Fred did with his electric guitar. Others wouldn't be too happy – Howlin' Wolf, who was born in 1910, once described his own 'modern' album, *New and Unimproved*, in which he was teamed with Jimi Hendrix-style rock musicians, as 'dogshit'. On the other hand, Buddy Guy (born 1936), a young showman who sang with the same kind of barely restrained hysterics as Robert Johnson, wanted to move in the Hendrix direction, but the same record company wouldn't let him. John Lee Hooker (born 1920), who faced similar pressures, was more philosophical. When he was teamed with The Vandellas vocal group and pushed into singing a version of the instrumental hit 'Green Onions', he commented wryly, 'I don't particularly like 'em, but say! the bread's good.'

But Mississippi blues are important enough to concentrate upon here for several reasons. One is the fact that the United States is a huge country and the blues seemed to occur almost simultaneously in vast areas – the equivalent, in Paul Oliver's memorable image, of a folk music developing at the same time in Copenhagen, London, Rome and Cairo. So there were important singers in several Texas cities, along the east coast in Georgia and the Carolinas, in other Deep South states, such as Alabama and Arkansas, and on the northern trail to Chicago and Detroit. Perhaps the blues originated in Mississippi – it seems likely, but remains unproven.

Even the name 'blues' is difficult to pin down – as far back as Elizabethan times the term was in use for depression, and an 1811 dictionary defines blue as 'to be confounded, terrified or disappointed, blue as a razor'. It also refers to the 'blue devils', a common term for low spirits, which appears in several blues and was the name of a jazz band led by Walter Page, and, intriguingly, to the term 'blue skin', for someone with mixed black and white parentage. No doubt these terms crossed the Atlantic with the early settlers. Even as late as the turn of the twentieth century, folk-song collectors found pure British folk music and archaic 16th-century English still in use in the isolated Appalachian mountains on America's East Coast. But early blues singers interviewed in recent years have often said they never called their music blues – the tunes they played in their youth were known as rags, reels, or simply dance music. The first mentions of blues as a musical form really date back to the early years of this century, and whether that was the same music that we now call blues is very likely, but not 100 per cent certain.

Yet despite the geographical diversity, the Mississippi blues came to represent the strongest and most dominant thread in the entire tapestry. It may be because they depended heavily on rhythmic impact, and therefore could be easily updated with the addition of bass and drums. It was certainly because so many Mississippians left the appalling conditions there and trekked to the northern cities looking for a better life, and took their music with them. And it was definitely due to the fact that if the blues is the foundation of western popular music, then the legacy of Mississippi is the bedrock beneath that foundation.

In the beginning was Son House, who in turn inspired Robert Johnson and Muddy Waters, and Johnson's spirit can be heard in the music of black followers, including Johnny Shines, Robert Lockwood, Elmore James, Homesick James, J. B. Hutto, and countless others. Johnson and Muddy Waters were also the direct inspiration of many white aspirants – Eric Clapton, Alexis Korner, and especially the Rolling Stones, who recorded Johnson's 'Love in Vain' with devotion. The young Elvis Presley loved the music of Mississippian Arthur Crudup and recorded his 'That's All Right Mama'; Bob Dylan tackled Bukka White's 'Fixin' to Die' and Tommy McClennan's 'Highway 51', while Elmore James' frenetic, electric updating of the Johnson sound was slavishly copied by every kid who could put a guitar and a slide together in some semblance of order. The essence of Mississippi blues lies at the heart of rock 'n' roll: an amalgam of blues, country music, boogie and novelty songs which swept the world. The most famous living blues veterans, B. B. King and John Lee Hooker, are both Mississippi men, as were the last generation of giants, men like Muddy Waters, Howlin' Wolf, Jimmy Rogers, Sonny Boy Williamson, Elmore James – the list is long and distinguished.

Perhaps it is a coincidence, but to leave it at that is being too simplistic. If you accept that the blues is a folk music, and that it has been governed in its development by social conditions as well as musical values, then Mississippi, and neighbouring Alabama, Arkansas and Louisiana, seem to have been destined by historical and cultural factors to be the places where the blues were toughest, angriest, and with a built-in crusading quality that was considerably safer than actually speaking out. Once the key to the blues is turned, the words of even the most innocuous song can have hidden meanings, subtleties which would mean a great deal to the listeners, but little to outsiders.

The blues from Georgia and the Carolinas were far removed from the churning self examination of the Delta singers. That's not to say they weren't as emotionally deep – Willie McTell, for instance, recorded some of the most moving and sensitive blues of all. It was just that he had a different way of doing it. And if you want entertainment, the vivacious dance numbers by Barbecue Bob Hicks are unrivalled, except perhaps by the rumbustious rags of Blind Boy Fuller from North Carolina, or the astonishing, almost miraculous, roller-coaster guitar of Blind Gary Davis from South Carolina, who single-handedly redefined what blues guitar was all about, even if he was singing mostly spirituals. I met him once and found him the most alien of them all, but certainly the most dynamic and gifted of all the pre-war veterans still performing.

But all these people come from the past and even Muddy, Wolf and Joe Williams (the epitome of the rambling bluesman) have gone now. Sleepy John Estes – a rare and lovely performer who everyone thought was ancient and dead until he was found, sounding as elderly as he had done in his youth – has gone, and so have Son, Bukka and Lightnin' Hopkins, the ultimate blues poet, as well as dear old Fred McDowell, cantankerous Furry Lewis (who inspired one of Joni Mitchell's best songs, 'Furry Sings The Blues'), God-ridden Robert Wilkins, and Skip James, the Messiah of the doomed.

So many who are part of history, and yet barely known outside the few who might buy their records because a song of theirs has been recorded, adapted and changed by some new pop idol. Thank God it still happens and the blues lives through the disciples who, in turn, encourage their own devotees to seek out the originals, even out of simple curiosity. For every Rolling Stones' fan who prefers Mick Jagger singing 'That's No Way to Get Along' to Robert Wilkins' original, there is another who learns what lies behind the second generation, and grows to love the first.

Today's blues heroes are very different to the older generation. They aren't necessarily black, although any attempt to kidnap the music and hold it to ransom, as that poor, benighted, *Blueprint* reader attempted, should be resisted at all costs. This is an essentially black music, as much as anything out of Soweto or Mali – or Hyderabad and Java, come to that. There is nothing to stop whites from borrowing it, in the same way that there are black crooners in the Sinatra/Bennett mode, or black groups who take The Beatles as a pattern. That is one of the joys of living in a shrinking world, and there is little music more exciting, more creative and exuberant, than the new blends of cultures and traditions. You can find traditional Irish music teamed with black gospel or Nashville in the records of De Danann and The Chieftains; an eclectic mix of jazz, blues and English folk in the work of Pentangle and the English Country Blues Band; a glorious melding of American tradition and Mali or India from Ry Cooder. How can the blues remain apart from this continuing fusion and reshaping?

The recordings of Robert Cray mentioned before are also a good example of how this century-old music has staked a claim to the 21st century. Cray doesn't often use traditional 12-bar

For sheer, blatant, unashamed sexuality, the records of Wynonie Harris are unbeatable. He sang raucous anthems of sex and drink with a hoarse cheerfulness that was totally endearing and sold many thousands of records. It was Harris who built a Loving Machine and ordered his woman not to roll those bloodshot eyes at him, and who took Roy Brown's 'Good Rockin' Tonight' into the charts long before Elvis Presley. He died of cancer in 1969.

PHOTOGRAPH: DAVID HAWKINS STUDIO

blues forms, yet his guitar work is firmly in the tradition, his songs are lyrically strong and intelligently argued, and their arrangements are based on the heavy, brass-punctuated, southern soul style deployed most successfully by singers identified with the Stax label. It's particularly interesting, because soul music appealed to younger blacks as a reaction against the old-fashioned blues which they felt represented a past of which they didn't want to be part.

Now Cray, Joe Louis Walker, Kenny Neal and others are using soul as a way to rejuvenate the blues, while Michael Hill, the most potentially exciting newcomer of 1994, manages to steer through Jimi Hendrix-style guitar pyrotechnics and African thumb piano while within easy mooring distance of the blues of the past century. More importantly, he is preaching the blues as a black achievement, an encouraging reversal of the rejection of the last generation. Others — on enthusiasts' labels such as Alligator, Black Top and Antones — also stick firmly to the traditional blues styles, but with the urgency and drive of rock music superimposed. As the blues changed from one man and a guitar or piano to small groups, from acoustic to electric, from folk music to big business, so it has survived. There are still people hammering out that timeless Elmore James riff, or hollering about standing at the crossroads trying to get a ride (there's even a singer called Blind Lemon Beefcake!), and there are several interesting white musicians, such as Chris Smither, Roy Bookbinder, Dave Peabody, Paul Geremia and Peter Nathanson, who plough a lonely furrow through the old-style country blues.

Amazingly, Mississippi is still turning out traditional-style bluesmen, albeit heavily influenced by records and radio, but singers like R. L. Burnside, Junior Kimbrough and CeDell Davis would have been right at home in the fifties, when the last great flowering of the old-fashioned, traditional country blues was recorded. Even better, they aren't, like so many white imitators, trying to recreate dusty museum pieces – their records reflect the music still heard in their own clubs and bars and dance halls today, and as such it has a validity and an importance which far transcends yet another Robert Johnson copy. The names and the music of the past echo down the years, and never has so much been available to hear on easily accessible CDs.

As the twentieth century draws to a close, so its most influential folk music flourishes in a way that scarcely seems credible, considering its roots and its original *raison d'être*. But whereas the words sung by Charley Patton, William Harris, Sam Collins and Bo Weavil Jackson were filled with dialect words, black patois and obscure figures of speech, the blues today speaks to everyone. Bobby Grant might sing about a nappy-haired woman coming through the mamlish corn, Frank Stokes might hymn his nehi woman and the Sparks Brothers muse on the merits of 4-11-44, but L'il Ed, Smokin' Joe Kubek, Michael Hill and the rest of the new breed of musicians who regard the blues as a proud legacy rather than a shameful reminder of a bitter past don't need the code words and the allusions – apart from the necessary street cred of the latest slang, of course. But that tends to be international, and understanding is limited by age, rather than race.

The new blues singers are citizens of the world, and the world still wants to hear the blues. The past, or much of it, is still available on record to hear and enjoy, to marvel at and revel in, as a wonderful, dynamic music removed from the social conditions that gave it birth. The present is different, but at heart still the same, and those of us who love the blues can only relish the dedication and the love that the young giants bring to keep the blues alive and developing. This book is dedicated both to them and also to the many others who don't appear in it. It will never be known what most of the early singers looked like, and they remain just a name on a record label and a handful of songs. It's a poor kind of immortality, but the best the world can offer them. Those who are featured here aren't necessarily the best or the most famous. This is a book of images, not another history of the blues, and the image of the blues is as well served by a superlative portrait of a comparative unknown as it is by yet another moody shot of the over-familiar few. Every blues singer adds something more to the breadth and depth of the music – here you will find the old, the young, the famous and the obscure, and, in this context, each is as important and as worth their place here as any other. Read the book, study these brief fleeting moments frozen on film, but most of all – listen to the music. That is where the real understanding of the blues lies.

plates

Mississippi street singer Ishmon (or Ishman on record) Bracey in the twenties, when he had a brief moment of fame as a recording artist for Victor and Paramount. He was closely associated with the influential Tommy Johnson, and his own records are a darker and coarser counterweight to Johnson's lighter and more delicate style. Bracey was rediscovered in the sixties, but had turned grimly to religion, and although he gave some useful information about the early blues, he never recorded again.

PHOTOGRAPH: COURTESY GAYLE DEAN WARDLOW

Blind Willie McTell, one of America's greatest folk musicians, pictured with his wife Kate in the thirties when McTell was recording for anyone who wanted him. He had a huge repertoire of elegiac blues, glorious ragtime dances, ballads and gospel (many with Kate singing with him), and his mastery of the clumsy 12-string guitar was unequalled. An intelligent, immensely talented musician, McTell stood at the pinnacle of the blues from the early twenties to his last informal session in 1956.

PHOTOGRAPH: COURTESY DAVID EVANS COLLECTION

Jimmy Yancey, one of the founding fathers of boogie woogie but of a quieter, more sensitive variety than Meade Lux Lewis and Albert Ammons. He was an influential figure in Chicago's jazz and blues circles, despite not recording until 1939, and was never a full-time musician. In his younger days as a tap dancer, he appeared with his father's vaudeville troupe at London's Buckingham Palace, but his long series of recordings in the forties remain a milestone of piano blues and boogie.

PHOTOGRAPH: COURTESY JOHN HOLLEY

It must have been a joke, posing Meade Lux Lewis with a book entitled *Practising the Piano*. Lewis was the master of boogie woogie, the train rhythm-driven, rollicking music that flowered in the twenties and had a big revival in the late thirties and early forties. Lewis' greatest contribution was 'Honky Tonk Train Blues', which stands with Pinetop's 'Boogie Woogie' and 'Yancey Special' as a foundation stone of the music. He died in a car crash in 1964.

PHOTOGRAPH: COURTESY BLUES UNLIMITED

The warm, smoky voice and pounding piano of Big Maceo Merriweather and the stinging guitar of Tampa Red made a wonderful partnership. Maceo influenced a whole generation of pianists, thanks to a driving style that married the bluesy sounds of Roosevelt Sykes and Leroy Carr with the boogie rhythms of Albert Ammons and Pete Johnson. 'Chicago Breakdown', 'Texas Stomp' and 'Macy Special' are enduring classics, but Maceo's career was cut short by a stroke in 1946 and his last few records are a sad testament to his illness.

PHOTOGRAPH: COURTESY BILL GREENSMITH

Hudson Whittaker (or Woodbridge), better known as Tampa Red, the 'Guitar Wizard', and the founding father of the hokum craze of the twenties. 'Tight Like That', his duet with Georgia Tom, sold thousands and rather overshadows his achievements as a slide guitar master, a musician able to adapt to changing styles and one equally happy in sensitive solo blues, bawdy party songs, jazz, sentimental pop and electric blues. A giant figure over more than 30 years.

PHOTOGRAPH: COURTESY BILL GREENSMITH

Josh White was a superb and influential guitarist in the light, East Coast style, but his polite, uninvolved vocals fail to excite many modern collectors. As a child, he guided blind singers such as Willie Walker and Joe Taggart, and his first recording was as accompanist to Taggart in 1928. He recorded dozens of blues and gospel sides throughout the thirties, before turning largely to folk and protest songs. He died in 1969, but his son, Josh White Jr., carries on the tradition.

PHOTOGRAPH: TERRY CRYER

A sensitive portrait of Huddie Ledbetter – 'Leadbelly' – a demonic figure in blues mythology who killed several men and sang his way out of prison. More importantly, he was a master of the clumsy 12-string guitar and a treasure house of American song of all kinds. The Leadbelly musical legacy stretches across 15 years to his death in 1949, and many of his songs, such as 'Good Night Irene', 'Black Girl' and 'Midnight Special', are still favourites today.

PHOTOGRAPH: COURTESY THE WESTON COLLECTION

Mance Lipscomb, a treasure house of old blues, ballads, folk songs, gospel, and any other kind of music that took his fancy. He spent most of his life farming in Texas and playing at weekends and at socials. He was first recorded when he was 65, and made five remarkable albums in a light melodic voice backed with intricate, finger-picked guitar. He also appeared in several blues documentaries before retiring from music in 1974. He died two years later, aged 81.

PHOTOGRAPH: CHRIS STRACHWITZ

Sam Chatmon, last of the Mississippi Sheiks and a survivor from before the blues was born, was a member of an extraordinary Mississippi musical family that included Bo Carter – one of the most widely recorded bluesmen of the thirties – and sometimes claimed the great Charley Patton as a half brother. After being rediscovered in 1960, he had a long and fruitful career as a songster, recording songs such as 'God Don't Like Ugly' and 'I Have to Paint my Face', as well as blues. He died in 1984, aged 87.

PHOTOGRAPH: TERRY JOHNSON

'I am the Black Ace, I'm the boss card in your hand' sang Texan Babe Karo Lemon 'Buck' Turner to the whine of a steel guitar played flat across his lap. Turner, a major bluesman, lamentably recorded just six issued sides before being rediscovered in 1960. He learned to play Hawaiian guitar from the great Oscar Woods – 'The Lone Wolf' – and the tradition was carried on in the fifties by Hop Wilson, but few others. A tragically under-recorded artist who died in 1972.

PHOTOGRAPH: COURTESY BILL GREENSMITH

The Reverend Rubin (or Reubin) Lacy, who, as Rube Lacy, recorded two seminal Mississippi blues in 1928 before quitting music to become a minister. He was even cheated out of payment on that one 78 and, although he is rumoured to play on other artists' records, he never recorded under his own name again.

Son House regarded Lacy as a major influence, and those two sides suggest a great potential that was never fully realized – a familiar story in the blues.

PHOTOGRAPH: DAVID EVANS

Eddie Son House, the archetypal Delta bluesman, in a relaxed moment from 1967 that belies his ferocious singing and aggressive slide guitar. His urgent, emotional vocals and percussive guitar were recorded in 1930 at a seminal session for Paramount with Charley Patton and Willie Brown, and the Library of Congress captured him at his peak in the early forties. He was rediscovered in 1964 and had a second career as the greatest surviving bluesman from the earliest days of the music.

PHOTOGRAPH: SYLVIA PITCHER

Veteran pianists Sunnyland Slim and Jimmy Walker outside Slim's shop in 1976. Slim started playing in the twenties, although he didn't record until 1947 (as Doctor Clayton's Buddy). He appeared on hundreds of records, either under his own name or as accompanist, and it was he who arranged Muddy Waters' first date at Chess. A raucous singer, dynamic pianist and the elder statesman of Chicago blues until his death in 1995.

PHOTOGRAPH: SYLVIA PITCHER

Buddy Moss might have succeeded Blind Boy Fuller as the premier East Coast bluesman, if a prison sentence for murder hadn't halted his career at its peak. He was born in Georgia and recorded with Curley Weaver and Barbecue Bob, as well as recording a long series of superb Piedmont blues. But after release from jail in 1941 his chance had gone, and he did little during the blues revival. He died in 1984, but appreciation of this important figure continues to grow.

PHOTOGRAPH: VAL WILMER

Alex Moore was an active pianist in the Dallas area of Texas for more than seven decades, although he recorded comparatively little. He was a fairly limited performer, sticking to the same few themes, but numbers such as 'West Texas Blues' and 'Blue Bloomer Blues' are evidence of his ability to blend blues and ragtime in a somewhat dated fashion. Spasmodic post-war recordings added little to his permanent legacy.

PHOTOGRAPH: BILL GREENSMITH

Sippie Wallace was a member of the musically talented Thomas family, which also included brothers George and Hersal. She recorded extensively throughout the twenties with jazz stars such as Louis Armstrong, Sidney Bechet and Johnny Dodds, and is one of the few classic blues singers whose records are worth having for the vocals as well as the accompaniment. She had a good second career in the sixties, recording a highly praised album with Bonnie Raitt. She died in 1986.

PHOTOGRAPH: SYLVIA PITCHER

A poignant picture of ruined majesty. Memphis Minnie, greatest of the women blues singers, in a nursing home after suffering a stroke. The picture on the cupboard shows her in her youth, when she cut hundreds of top-class records, especially a long series of highly acclaimed duets with her then partner, Kansas Joe McCoy. It was moving pictures such as this in *Blues Unlimited* magazine that alerted fans to her plight and gained her some financial support in the sad last years when the fame and fortune had vanished.

PHOTOGRAPH: COURTESY BLUES UNLIMITED

He was cantankerous and crotchety at times, but Furry Lewis was usually willing to play for visitors for a fee. He recorded some fine blues and ballads in the twenties, after working in minstrel shows and on street corners. Despite losing a leg, he was a street cleaner in Memphis for more than 40 years, as well as appearing in a Burt Reynolds film and even in *Playboy* magazine. He remained on top form as bluesman, showman and storyteller until his death in 1981.

PHOTOGRAPH: AXEL KÜSTNER

Booker Washington White, better known as 'Bukka', and one of the finest Mississippi bluesmen of all. He recorded with Memphis Minnie in 1930, but his real legacy was a series of bitter, sensitive and deeply personal songs made in 1940 after a painful period in Parchman Farm jail for murder. He was rediscovered in 1963 – a year after Bob Dylan recorded his song 'Fixin' to Die' on his debut album – and had a fitful career on the white folk circuit. He died in 1977.

PHOTOGRAPH: SYLVIA PITCHER

Gus Cannon, pictured here in 1971, is best known to the general world, if at all, as the writer of the Rooftop Singers' 1963 chart topper, 'Walk Right In'. Yet he was born in 1883 and led the finest and most innovative of all the Memphis jug bands, Cannon's Jug Stompers, which recorded minstrel songs, blues, rags and dances. In later years, he appeared in films and festivals and even recorded for the leading soul label, Stax. He died aged 96, ending a link with the music of more than a century ago.

PHOTOGRAPH: VAL WILMER

'If I get lucky, mama', hollered Arthur 'Big Boy' Crudup in 1941 – and he did. He came up from Mississippi, and his first records are simple, timeless country blues with vivid imagery, sung in a high, floating style that was generations old.

His later, more modern, sides influenced numerous other singers, such as the young Elvis Presley, whose first records included Crudup's 'That's All Right Mama'. He had a second career as a country blues singer for white audiences before his death in 1974.

PHOTOGRAPH: SYLVIA PITCHER

David 'Honeyboy' Edwards was one of the Mississippi singers who never really got the breaks. He recorded impressively for the Library of Congress in 1942, but his handful of commercial recordings remained largely unissued until the LP era. Edwards is one of the few remaining links with Robert Johnson, Tommy McClennan and other Mississippi giants, which has tended to overshadow his own quirky, archaic style. He is pictured recording for a BBC *Blues on Two* television programme in Manchester, England.

PHOTOGRAPH: DAVE PEABODY

'Speckled Red', the working name of raucous piano player and singer Rufus Perryman, whose cleaned-up, 1929 recording of the obscene 'The Dirty Dozen' was a major hit. He failed to follow it up with any other big sellers, though, and even after he was rediscovered playing in small bars in 1954, he failed to emulate the fame of his brother, Willie ('Piano Red') who, ironically, had a huge success with a rocking fifties update of Speckled Red's 1930 song, 'The Right String But The Wrong Yo Yo'.

PHOTOGRAPH: TERRY CRYER

Aaron 'T-Bone' Walker and 'Big Mama' Willie Mae Thornton, two different branches of the blues. Walker first recorded obscurely in 1929, but went on to become the most influential electric guitarist in the music, combining a feel for jazz and considerable showmanship. His most famous song, recorded by many others, was 'Stormy Monday'. Big Mama was a hell-raising blues shouter with a gravelly edge who first recorded the Elvis Presley hit, 'Hound Dog', and Janis Joplin's showstopper, 'Ball 'n' Chain'. A formidable descendant of Bessie Smith and Memphis Minnie.

PHOTOGRAPH: BILL GREENSMITH

Two generations of the blues, pictured in 1976. Margie Evans used to sing with the Johnny Otis Show, before striking out on her own with albums biased towards jazz and funk rather than blues. Lowell Fulson first recorded a mixture of acoustic country duets and small-group city blues in the forties, before moving up to full-scale band blues. An interesting and diverse performer, who appears equally at home in any field and whose popularity seems secure.

PHOTOGRAPH: VAL WILMER

John Jackson, one of the last of the old-time songsters, spent much of his working life as a gravedigger, playing at weekends and at social functions. Like Mance Lipscomb from Texas and Jesse Fuller from Georgia, Virginian Jackson is a storehouse of American songs, ranging from full-scale ballads, through rags and country music, to blues. He first recorded in 1965, and has since made hundreds of sides and toured Europe with great success. He might have been a major star, but chose to remain at home.

PHOTOGRAPH: SYLVIA PITCHER

Everyone enjoys Jesse Fuller's affable brand of one-man band music, dances, blues, hokum and vaudeville. He invented an instrument called the fotdella, a home-made bass with piano strings played with a foot pedal, which, with the addition of hi-hat, harmonica, kazoo and 12-string guitar, gave an extraordinarily full sound. A Jesse Fuller concert might include his biggest hit, 'San Francisco Bay Blues', but also old-time spirituals, pop songs, imitation work songs, jazz standards, and even vaudeville numbers. He died in 1976, a much-loved and respected songster.

PHOTOGRAPH: VAL WILMER

Robert 'Baby Boy' Warren played in the Detroit clubs with John Lee Hooker and Bobo Jenkins in the immediate post-war years. Hooker and Eddie Kirkland moved on, but Warren remained in Detroit, working in the car plants by day and as a musician by night. His reputation rests on just 19 records cut in the early fifties, all of which have become cherished collectors' items. He rarely toured because of his job, but did play in Europe in 1972. He died five years later.

PHOTOGRAPH: COURTESY BLUES UNLIMITED

Lonesome Sundown was the name chosen for Cornelius Green by Louisiana record producer Jay Miller, who also picked Lightnin' Slim, Slim Harpo and Lazy Lester. Sundown began his career with Clifton Chenier's zydeco band, but from 1956 to 1964 he made an album and 16 singles for Miller and Excello records. He gave up music for the church, and although he was persuaded to record another album in 1977, lack of success turned him away from music again.

PHOTOGRAPH: GERHARD ROBS

For thousands of people, the first experience of real blues singers was a concert by Sonny Terry and Brownie McGhee. Their durable partnership started after the death in 1941 of Sonny's previous partner, Blind Boy Fuller, and lasted, on and off, until 1975. The eerie sound of Terry's falsetto hollers and dog and train imitations on harmonica carried him from clubs to concert halls, and even into a Broadway musical. He died in 1986, and the urbane McGhee has retired.

PHOTOGRAPH: TERRY CRYER

Big Bill Broonzy loved to be regarded as the last of the great blues singers, but his contribution to the blues can scarcely be measured. From his early ragtime solos, through the hokum craze and the urbanization of the blues in the thirties, to the early beginnings of the folk-blues revival, Big Bill was a vital, central figure. A highly coloured and enormously entertaining 'autobiography' was put together from his letters, but his hundreds of records stand as his real memorial.

PHOTOGRAPH: TERRY CRYER

John 'Bobo' Jenkins was a club favourite in post-war Detroit, along with 'Baby Boy' Warren, Eddie Kirkland and John Lee Hooker, among others, but real success eluded him. He was an ex-gospel singer from Alabama before settling in Detroit, and although he recorded for Chess and Fortune, he failed to make any impact outside the city. He even set up his own company, Big Star, but remained a minor figure until his death in 1984.

PHOTOGRAPH: COURTESY BOBO JENKINS

Elmore James' shy exterior belied his reputation as the single most important post-war slide guitarist. He took the music of Robert Johnson, electrified it, and developed an instantly recognizable sound that spawned countless imitators. His anguished, tortured vocals and violent guitar riffs made him sound as if he was living every blues ever sung and, at his best, he represents the sound of the city in a way that overshadows even Muddy Waters and Howlin' Wolf. He died in 1963, virtually unknown to white audiences, but his reputation grows yearly.

PHOTOGRAPH: COURTESY BILL GREENSMITH

While other bluesmen fell before the onslaught of rock 'n' roll, Big Joe Turner fought back by joining in. After a superb series of records with boogie pianist Pete Johnson, Turner relaunched his career with such rock classics as 'Shake Rattle and Roll', 'Flip Flop and Fly' and 'Honey Hush', which kept him on top. A major figure in the transition between rhythm and blues and rock in the years 1951–56, he even toured in rock 'n' roll package tours as a kind of father figure. This picture was taken in 1974, eleven years before his death.

PHOTOGRAPH: BILL GREENSMITH

'Little Brother' Eurreal Montgomery, pictured here at London's 100 Club in 1961, came out of the logging camps and brothels to record some of the most enduring barrelhouse piano and songs, such as 'Vicksburg Blues' and 'No Special Rider'. A man blessed with a good memory, he provided the few details that are known today of many otherwise forgotten backwoods' pianists. He recorded heavily, and even had his own label in the sixties. He died in 1985, still a formidable musician.

PHOTOGRAPH: VAL WILMER

'Mr Five by Five' was the apt nickname for roly-poly Jimmy Rushing, a small man with a huge voice that could be heard over a big band. He sang (but never recorded) with Jelly Roll Morton in the twenties before joining Walter Page's Blue Devils and Bennie Moten's Orchestra. His great years, however, were with Count Basie from 1935 to 1950, when he recorded a fair number of durable classics. He died in 1972.

PHOTOGRAPH: TERRY CRYER

'Champion' Jack Dupree, reflecting in Cologne in 1983 on a long career that took him from New Orleans to Europe. A former boxing champion, Dupree first recorded in 1940 as a two-fisted barrelhouse player. He was a rhythm and blues star in New York in the fifties, but moved to Europe to escape prejudice, making hundreds of records before his death in 1992. More of a comic entertainer than a serious bluesman, but a major figure in both fields.

PHOTOGRAPH: AXEL KÜSTNER

Watching Mississippi Fred McDowell perform was like seeing
the history of the blues come alive. Although he didn't record
until 1959, his music was rooted in the style of Son House
and Charley Patton. He was discovered by chance on an
Alan Lomax field trip and, happily, was widely recorded as
a slide-guitar soloist of enormous power and invention, as an
accompanist to gospel singers and blues shouter Big Mama
Thornton, and as an electric guitarist. His recorded legacy –
ended with his death in 1972 – is extensive and important.
PHOTOGRAPH: VAL WILMER

The Reverend Gary Davis, cigar at a jaunty angle, demonstrating his skills on an ungainly 12-string guitar. Davis, a blind street preacher from South Carolina, was one of the finest guitarists ever to record and a major influence on East Coast singers such as Blind Boy Fuller. Sadly, he recorded only a handful of blues, but his fiery gospel songs and elegant ragtime dances remain among the most enduring delights of black American music. He died in 1972, leaving a magnificent recorded legacy.

PHOTOGRAPH: SYLVIA PITCHER

Jimmy Witherspoon, pictured
here at a jazz festival in 1964,
made his name with Jay
McShann's band, where the
saxophonist was a young
Charlie Parker. His rich, dark
voice is bluesier than other
shouters, such as Joe Turner or
Jimmy Rushing, and his
reworking of Bessie Smith's
'T'aint Nobody's Business' was
in the 1949 hit parade for 34
weeks. His records since then
top the thousand mark, despite
his being unable to adapt to the
new rock 'n' roll, and
Witherspoon has stayed firmly
in the jazz vocalist mode.
PHOTOGRAPH: VAL WILMER

Bobby 'Blue' Bland was one of
a group of singers – Ray
Charles and Sam Cooke were
others – who blended blues and
gospel into a fevered new form
which some call soul-blues. He
was a member of the Beale
Streeters in Memphis, with
B. B. King, Rosco Gordon,
Johnny Ace and others, but his
career took off with a post-army
contract with Duke Records
which saw numerous big hits. A
major influence on many rock
singers, Bland remains a
formidable figure.
PHOTOGRAPH: SYLVIA PITCHER

Big Joe Williams, pictured in his home town of
Crawford, Mississippi, in 1978, was the archetypal
wandering bluesman – roaming the south, hopping
freight trains, and dodging the law. He played
anywhere that wanted a musician, and even developed
a unique nine-string guitar to give him the big sound he
wanted. He recorded widely and well and was a great
favourite on the concert circuit. A hugely talented
musician, whose songs included the much-recorded
'Baby Please Don't Go', he died in 1982.

PHOTOGRAPH: AXEL KÜSTNER

Louisiana Red (right), the chameleon of the blues,
also known as Rocky Fuller, Playboy Fuller, Rockin'
Red and L. A. Red. His real name is Iverson Minter,
and all that name changing did little to bring him
much success. He lives in Europe and is a regular
festival performer. On the left is James 'Son'
Thomas, an excellent Mississippi Delta singer-
guitarist made famous by writer William Ferris; he
toured Europe several times and appeared in film
documentaries. He died in 1993.

PHOTOGRAPH: AXEL KÜSTNER

Looking just like the King Bee about which he sang, this is Slim Harpo, one of the two greatest swamp blues singers and the one who most influenced the British rhythm and blues boom. His attractive, nasal voice and laid-back, lolloping rhythms contrasted beautifully with Lightnin' Slim's rougher drawl, giving producer Jay Miller a varied pair of hit makers. Slim Harpo played at several rock concerts before dying aged 46 in 1970, but his timeless music is more popular than ever.

PHOTOGRAPH: COURTESY BLUES UNLIMITED

Jimmy Reed sold more records than any other post-war bluesman, yet he was the most basic and least adventurous of any. His lazy, laid back vocals, slurred delivery, catchy tunes and rolling rhythms caught the spirit of the blues revival perfectly. He had an enormous string of hits in both the blues and pop field, and it is the Reed sound that is the basis of the swamp blues of Slim Harpo, Jimmy Anderson, Lazy Lester and others. A most unlikely pop hero, he died in 1976.

PHOTOGRAPH: BRIAN SMITH

Howlin' Wolf was a giant of a man, with a ferocious voice and a delivery to match. To see him in action was one of the greatest experiences the blues could offer – and even his greatest records barely hint at his overwhelming presence and frightening intensity. He came out of Mississippi – his vocals echo the hard-edged, throat-ripping style of Charley Patton – to make his name in Memphis and then Chicago. He was a terrifying, uncompromising figure who generated a mesmerizing hypnotic power like no other.

PHOTOGRAPH: SYLVIA PITCHER

Eddie Taylor is best known as Jimmy Reed's guitarist – which is a pity. For if Reed found the simple formula for a string of hits – catchy tunes, sleepy vocals – Taylor was a far superior musician, as his handful of solo sides show. It's also Taylor's guitar that lifts Reed's records out of the ordinary and stops them sinking under their own banality. He was much in demand as a guitarist after Reed died, and recorded some pleasant albums before his own death in 1985.

PHOTOGRAPH: BILL GREENSMITH

Otis Spann spent his early years playing piano in Mississippi juke joints, fighting as a professional boxer and competing in semi-professional football. He moved to Chicago in 1951, and appeared on numerous Chess recordings by Howlin' Wolf, Little Walter and – particularly – Muddy Waters, in whose band he became a vital component. He also had a good solo career, recording for a number of labels, both with and without the Waters band. He died in 1970, at the early age of 40.

PHOTOGRAPH: COURTESY BLUES UNLIMITED

Muddy Waters' first recordings were brilliant country blues, cut for the Library of Congress in 1941 and later revived at the start of his long recording career for Chess. It was Waters – real name McKinley Morganfield – who dressed up the old Mississippi blues in a new suit and hat and moved them to Chicago. Like Robert Johnson, he was a catalyst, melding the old and the new. His bands employed virtually every Chicago star, and his music remains as the finest flowering of the blues in the city. He died in 1983.

PHOTOGRAPH: SYLVIA PITCHER

A sensitive study in 1963 of Lonnie Johnson, one of the greatest blues and jazz guitarists – ever. He was equally at home playing with Louis Armstrong and Duke Ellington, backing rough country singers such as Texas Alexander, or recording dazzling, dancing duets with white guitarist Eddie Lang. A nasal, pervasive vocalist, his guitar playing remains one of the wonders of the age. The picture was taken at the famous Marquee Club, in London's Oxford Street.

PHOTOGRAPH: VAL WILMER

Memphis Slim, American Ambassador-At-Large of Good Will and a French Commander of Arts and Letters – singular honours for a piano-playing bluesman from Tennessee. Slim – real name Peter Chatman – was a major part of the Chicago scene before the war and recorded widely before making a wise move to France, where he was able to work and record while bluesmen back home were finding times hard. He died in 1988, too familiar and accessible to be regarded as a top-line bluesman by many collectors.

PHOTOGRAPH: SYLVIA PITCHER

'Harmonica' Phil Wiggins and 'Bowling Green'
John Cephas are among the few who still keep
the spirit of the old acoustic Piedmont blues
alive. They met in 1976, and played with
barrelhouse pianist 'Big Chief' Ellis in the
Barrelhouse Rockers until Ellis' death. Since then
they have been a duo, carrying the raggy sound
of the East Coast states across the world and
beating electric bluesmen to major awards.
Deliberate archaism, perhaps, but far more than
just dusty museum music.

PHOTOGRAPH: SYLVIA PITCHER

James Cotton, one of the most important post-war harmonica players, here playing with the Chris Barber band in 1961. In 1954, he recorded for Sun with guitarist Pat Hare, and produced 'Cotton Crop Blues', a distorted, angry masterpiece which remains one of the true classics of post-war blues. His work in one of the best Muddy Waters bands boosted his reputation and he has recorded and toured widely. Cotton remains a much-respected figure on the blues circuit.

PHOTOGRAPH: VAL WILMER

One of the mysteries of the blues is why Weldon 'Juke Boy' Bonner never made the big time. He was a skilled multi-instrumentalist, a strong, gritty singer, and a songwriter of perception and vision, venturing far beyond the usual themes with his heartfelt protests about racial prejudice and poverty. Yet apart from a European tour, and despite strong championship from a small body of fans, his life ended in 1988, with Bonner bitter and poor. A much under-rated talent, pictured here in 1976.

PHOTOGRAPH: AXEL KÜSTNER

Like so many others, Eddie Boyd came up from the Mississippi Delta to make his name in the post-war blues capital of Chicago, where he worked with Muddy Waters, Johnny Shines and John Lee 'Sonny Boy' Williamson. Recordings with saxophonist J. T. Brown's band got him his own contract, and big hits with 'Five Long Years', 'Third Degree' and '24 Hours'. Success on European tours persuaded him to move, first to Paris, then Finland, where he turned to gospel music until his death in 1994.

PHOTOGRAPH: AXEL KÜSTNER

Katie Webster was a regular
member of Otis Redding's revue,
but she is also one of the unsung
heroines of the blues. She
reckons she played on around
500 singles in the fifties and
sixties, although she made few
recordings under her own name.
A two-fisted pianist in the
barrelhouse style, she also
recorded the odd pop ballad,
but her best work is probably as
a session musician behind such
luminaries as Slim Harpo,
Lightnin' Slim and Lazy Lester.
Recent recordings show she has
lost none of her power.
PHOTOGRAPH: PAUL NATKIN

Koko Taylor may be the last of
the women blues shouters, now
that Big Mama Thornton and
Big Maybelle have gone. Her
record of Willie Dixon's fruity
'Wang Wang Doodle' was a
huge seller, and by the end of
the eighties she had won an
astonishing ten W. C. Handy
awards – more than any other
blues artist. She even performed
for President Bush. A long series
of excellent albums for Alligator
and a hectic touring and concert
schedule have kept her
reputation secure.
PHOTOGRAPH: COURTESY BLUES UNLIMITED

Lightnin' Slim (Otis Hicks), epitome of the swamp bluesman. He was a limited guitarist, but his slow, lazy drawl, which sounded as if he had been dredged up from a Louisiana swamp, generated one of the rawest, most blues-drenched sounds of the post-war years. Lightnin' was discovered by Louisiana record producer Jay Miller, who went on to record other swamp bluesmen, such as Slim Harpo, Lazy Lester and Lonesome Sundown. But Lightnin' Slim, who died in 1974, was always the best.

PHOTOGRAPH: SYLVIA PITCHER

Frank Frost is one of many local musicians who have gained considerable fame in collecting circles, but have failed to make their mark in the wider world. He learned to play harmonica from Sonny Boy Williamson (Aleck Miller), although he actually played guitar in Williamson's band in the fifties. Frost is a member of the Jelly Roll Kings, who made a much-praised album for Sun founder Sam Phillips in 1963. Frost has toured Europe, but generally remains a mainstay of the Delta juke joints.

PHOTOGRAPH: KEVIN REYNOLDS

A relaxed moment for three stalwarts of Chicago blues. On the left is Fred
Below, the drummer whose jazzy backbeat enlivened countless blues
records by the biggest names on the Chess roster. He died in 1988.
Centre is Jimmy Lee Robinson, one of the many footnotes in the history of
the music and a minor name in this august company. On the right is Snooky
Pryor, one of the first and most influential of the post-war Chicago players
and still an effective performer.

PHOTOGRAPH: BILL GREENSMITH

Brothers Louis (left) and David Myers (above) began by playing
at house rent parties in Chicago, where they met Junior Wells.
Together they formed The Aces, one of the city's finest electric
blues bands, which was later taken over by Little Walter and
renamed The Jukes. Both men remained regular performers,
playing and recording with numerous stars, although ill health
handicapped Louis' activities before his death in 1994.

PHOTOGRAPHS: SYLVIA PITCHER (ABOVE); BILL GREENSMITH (LEFT)

Little Walter, an aggressive and quarrelsome character murdered in 1968 in a street brawl, was the greatest and most influential of the post-war harmonica players. He came from Louisiana, and his early work partnering Muddy Waters has never been equalled for sheer beauty and lyric elegance. He made a long series of recordings that were initially imbued with creativity and vivid inventions, but which sadly deteriorated as drink and a fiery temperament took the upper hand. He, if anyone, was the flawed genius of the blues.
PHOTOGRAPH: BRIAN SMITH

Aleck Rice Miller claimed to be the original Sonny Boy Williamson, but was certainly the second on record after John Lee Williamson. Many of his songs, such as 'Eyesight to the Blind' and 'Nine Below Zero', have become enduring classics. Sadly, he didn't record until 1951, although he had been a radio star for ten years, but the results were glorious, rough-and-ready juke-joint music. He went on to be a star of Chess records in Chicago and a great favourite of European audiences before his lonely death in 1980.
PHOTOGRAPH: COURTESY BLUES UNLIMITED

Professor Longhair (Henry Roeland – Roy – Byrd) shows London's Carnaby Street what snappy dressing is really all about in 1973. Longhair was one of the most eccentric musicians in the blues, offering an enticing mix of all the different kinds of music to be found in New Orleans and Louisiana. Fats Domino learned from him, and so did Dr John and many others. His 'Mardi Gras in New Orleans' is still the anthem of the festival. Byrd died in 1980.

PHOTOGRAPH: PARKER A. DINKINS

The familiar pork pie hat crowns Roosevelt Sykes, a seminal pianist and talent scout in St Louis and Chicago before the war, pictured here in happy mood in 1973. Sykes was a majestic singer and influential musician, and recorded many hundreds of sides in his long career. Sharing the joke are 'Cousin Joe' (Pleasant Joseph), left, a much under-rated New Orleans singer-pianist with a witty song-writing style, and Reverend Gatemouth Moore, now a minister but a solid rhythm and blues vocalist in the late forties.

PHOTOGRAPH: VAL WILMER

Like everyone associated with Robert Johnson, Johnny Shines found people less interested in him than in his relationship with his mentor. Yet he was a superb singer with a rich, intense vibrato, and his shimmering slide guitar was magnificent. He gave up music when no one seemed interested in his old-fashioned style, but took it up again in 1965 and toured far and wide, preaching the Delta blues. A stroke in 1980 caused playing problems, but he continued performing until his death in 1992.

PHOTOGRAPH: DAVE PEABODY

Robert Pete Williams, one of the few genuinely unique bluesmen, was discovered by folklorist Harry Oster in Louisiana's notorious Angola Prison, where he was serving time for murder. His music seemed to obey no formal rules, with curious timing and rhythms, while his lyrics were personal and often deeply moving. In time-honoured fashion, his singing got him released from jail and he performed and recorded widely, albeit not so successfully as easier, less demanding singers. He died in 1980.

PHOTOGRAPH: SYLVIA PITCHER

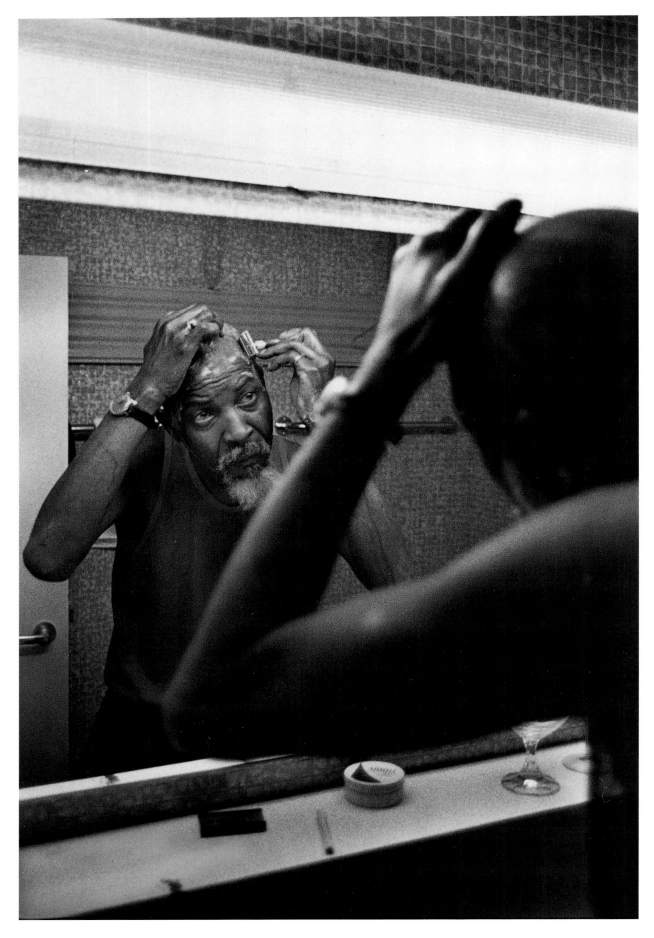

Eddie 'Cleanhead' Vinson owes more to jazz than blues, although his blues shouting has as many fans as his screaming alto sax playing. He was born in Texas in 1917, and got his nickname after an attempt to straighten his hair caused it all to fall out. He played with T-Bone Walker in the thirties, and with the Milt Larkin and Cootie Williams orchestras, before starting his own band in 1945. He made a long series of recordings before his death in 1988.

PHOTOGRAPH: VAL WILMER

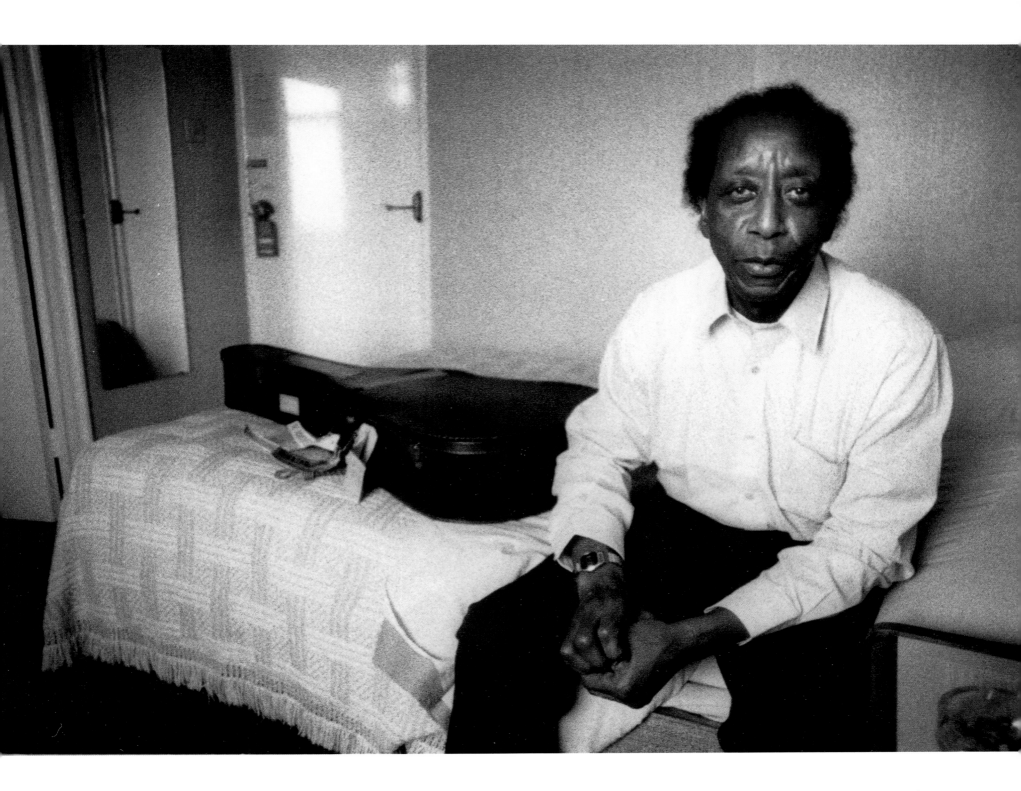

One-man bands aren't too common in the blues, but Dr Isaiah Ross was the finest of them all. A Mississippi musician, his music is rooted in the sound of Sonny Boy Williamson and John Lee Hooker, but with the overlay of boogie rhythms and the ability to sound like a complete band all by himself. His fifties recordings for the Sun label are finally being issued and are justly collectors' items, but his most developed work is on albums for Testament and Blue Horizon. He died in 1993.

PHOTOGRAPH: MARC MARNIE

Sam 'Lightnin'' Hopkins, the blues' greatest poet, could walk into a studio and record a song on the spot when he needed money for a drink. When young, he played with Blind Lemon Jefferson and Texas Alexander (his cousin), and made his first records in 1946 with pianist Wilson 'Thunder' Smith – hence his nickname. His music ranges from the rawest country blues to raucous, small-band, dance-hall sides, and he recorded more than almost any other post-war bluesman. One of America's greatest folk musicians, he died of cancer in 1982.

PHOTOGRAPH: DOUG FULTON

The great John Lee Hooker, master of the hard, driven boogie and the blackest blues, in action before he became a Grand Old Man of the music. His earliest recordings, from the late forties and early fifties, were masterpieces of Mississippi Delta blues, updated and electrified for a city audience. These days, after some years of neglect, he is enjoying a remarkable Indian Summer as a major star with young admirers flocking to record with him. As one of his biggest selling albums dubbed him, he really is 'Mr Lucky'.

PHOTOGRAPHS: SYLVIA PITCHER

J. B. Hutto (left) and Hound Dog Taylor with band members Brewer Phillips and Ted Harvey outside Florence's Lounge, Chicago. Both Hutto and Taylor were slide guitarists in the frenetic Elmore James style: both were more concerned with effect than innovation, and both were very exciting indeed at their best. Hutto, whose early records are ferocious masterpieces, was the uncle of highly promising young bluesman L'il Ed. He died in 1987. Taylor, a coarse, unschooled, but highly charged player, recorded three superb albums before his death in 1975.

PHOTOGRAPH: COURTESY BLUES UNLIMITED

Carey Bell is another Mississippian who made his name in the Chicago blues bands, although his first record was made in London in 1969. He has never made the really big time, although his work on the chromatic harmonica echoes that of Little Walter and Walter Horton. He toured with Willie Dixon, and with his own band, which included his guitarist son, Lurrie. Bell has a small – but vocal – following, especially in Europe.

PHOTOGRAPH: SYLVIA PITCHER

Riley B. King, better known as 'B. B.', and probably the best-known living bluesman. He's yet another with Mississippi roots, and the one with the greatest influence on rock guitarists, from Eric Clapton to Stevie Ray Vaughan. King is a cousin of pre-war blues master Bukka White, who helped get him started and watched him gain the kind of fame denied himself. B. B. has made hundreds of records, but his *Live at the Regal* set is usually named as the finest live blues recording ever made.

PHOTOGRAPH: SYLVIA PITCHER

A wistful study of Big Walter 'Shaky' Horton, one of the major post-war harmonica stylists. Born in Mississippi, he performed with the Memphis Jug Band, but made his first records for Sun in Memphis, including 'Easy', a remarkable duet with guitarist Jimmy de Berry which is so imaginative and unique it has inspired entire critical articles. He never regained those heights, but was a first-rate sideman in many of the great Chicago bands, including those led by Muddy Waters, Jimmy Rogers and Howlin' Wolf. He died in 1981.

PHOTOGRAPH: SYLVIA PITCHER

Earl Hooker's reputation as one of the finest slide guitarists in post-war Chicago is hardly ever justified by his records. He rarely sang, concentrating on instrumentals, which probably denied him the fame of his cousin, John Lee Hooker. His first recordings for King and Sun (largely unissued until recently), are collectors' items, but most of his considerable recorded legacy suggests only a journeyman musician. He might have broken into the big time with help from rock-guitarist fan Duane Allman, but he died of TB in 1970, aged 40.
PHOTOGRAPH: VAL WILMER

A quiet moment in London in 1963 for Texas pianist Curtis Jones and singer Madeleine Bell. Jones recorded widely in the thirties and forties, but his lightly structured piano and anonymous voice inspire little interest today. He died in 1971, nine years after moving to France and enjoying a prosperous career in Europe. Madeleine Bell, once the only female member of the Alex Bradford Singers in Newark, New Jersey, later found success with the pop group Blue Mink.
PHOTOGRAPH: VAL WILMER

Johnny Young was a fairly minor figure on the post-war Chicago scene, although he was one of the first to record in 1947. He played mandolin on street corners for tips and in the clubs, but didn't record anything between 1948 and 1964. Plenty of sessions followed, including a jolly, affectionate album for Testament that recreated the sound of the thirties string bands, and he appeared at many festivals and college concerts. But he remained in the second rank until his death in 1974.

PHOTOGRAPH: SYLVIA PITCHER

Robert 'Junior' Lockwood, with a beautifully decorated resonator guitar at the 1994 Belgian Rhythm 'n' Blues Festival. Like Johnny Shines and Honeyboy Edwards, Lockwood remains overshadowed by Robert Johnson – his stepfather – who taught him to play guitar. A rather passionless singer but an inventive guitarist with leanings towards jazz, Lockwood has been a stalwart of the Chicago club and recording scene since the fifties, and remains a festival favourite. The continuing interest in Johnson has done him no harm at all.

PHOTOGRAPH: DAVE PEABODY

Jimmy McCracklin has recorded an amazing number of sides, several of which even crossed over into the pop charts. He was a major rhythm and blues artist in California after the Second World War, tackling everything from straight blues to big-band jazz with equal aplomb. But his biggest success was a novelty number, 'The Walk', which he reportedly made to prove that anyone could write a rock 'n' roll hit! He is pictured at London's 100 Club in 1981.

PHOTOGRAPH: DAVE PEABODY

A wry look from Johnny Littlejohn, another of the many whose talents were not fully recognized. He came up from Mississippi to Chicago with a rough-edged voice and a slide guitar straight out of the Elmore James schoolbook. He played the clubs, made a couple of powerful albums and a short session for Chess (originally unissued), but failed to get that lucky break before his death in 1994.

PHOTOGRAPH: BILL GREENSMITH

'Magic Sam' Maghett was one of the Big Three of West Side Chicago blues, alongside Otis Rush and Buddy Guy, but a tragically early death curtailed a blossoming career. Another Mississippi Delta musician, he played in the 'Homesick' James Williamson band before gaining his own recording contract. A memorable and happily recorded set at the Ann Arbor Festival, Michigan, brought him numerous bookings in America and Europe, but he died too soon to take them up. He was 32.

PHOTOGRAPH: SYLVIA PITCHER

British blues critic Chris Smith memorably described Victoria Spivey (pictured in Croydon, England, in 1963) as the 'Madonna of the blues' because of her confident belief in her own talents, her string-pulling to get work for other women artists, and her constant themes of drugs, violence and off-beat sex. She recorded extensively between 1926 and 1937, and appeared in the all-black movie *Hallelujah!* and several stage musicals. In 1962, she formed Spivey Records to showcase surviving classic blues singers. She died in 1976.

PHOTOGRAPH: VAL WILMER

Otis Rush made one of the all-time classic Chicago blues records ('I Can't Quit You Baby') and one of the worst ('Violent Love'). One of the three most important West Side Chicago guitarists of the fifties (the others were Magic Sam and Buddy Guy), Rush has, perhaps, never fulfiled his early promise. Another Mississippian, he started recording in 1956, and his sides for the Cobra label remain definitive statements. Since then, success has been sparse, despite an attempt to emulate the John Lee Hooker star album format.

PHOTOGRAPH: SYLVIA PITCHER

Albert King was a Mississippi bluesman whose career was boosted into orbit by the specialist soul label Stax. He played left handed with his guitar upside down, and his single-string playing emphasized a distinctive bent-note approach. Early records meant little, but a contract with Stax, and records with Booker T. and the MGs – combining blues with brass-laden southern soul – made King a world star. He went on to record with a symphony orchestra and headline rock concerts. He died in 1992.

PHOTOGRAPH: SYLVIA PITCHER

Junior Wells, probably best known for his enduring partnership with Buddy Guy, was one of the founding fathers of the Chicago blues harmonica style. Strongly influenced by Little Walter and Sonny Boy Williamson, he made his name with Louis Myers and Muddy Waters before striking out on his own. International success came with an album with Buddy Guy for the Delmark label, and he went on to record with Eric Clapton, Dr John and Rolling Stone Bill Wyman, among others.

PHOTOGRAPH: SYLVIA PITCHER

If anyone captured the scarcely controlled hysteria of Robert Johnson's style in post-war years, it was Buddy Guy. Guy came from Louisiana, where he made two very restrained records, to rewrite blues guitar in Chicago. His single-string guitar solos may have been influenced by B. B. King, but his vocals – hoarse, impassioned, wailing with all the fervour of a hot gospeller – suggested the way Johnson might have gone had he lived. History will probably judge Guy on the basis of his magnificent, emotionally charged sides for Chess between 1960–67.

PHOTOGRAPHS: SYLVIA PITCHER

Floyd Jones and his cousin Moody were among the earliest musicians who reformed the music of the Mississippi Delta into the hard-edged, post-war Chicago band sound. Guitarist Floyd was a melancholy singer who specialized in songs about hard times and blighted ambition, but they are justifiably highly regarded by collectors. Floyd was never a full-time musician and rarely left Chicago, which is possibly why he is less well-known outside specialist circles than he deserves.

PHOTOGRAPH: FRANK SCOTT

Billy Boy Arnold, another of the many journeymen musicians who make up the history of the blues. He was strongly influenced by Sonny Boy Williamson, Little Walter and Junior Wells, and never really developed a recognizable sound of his own. He recorded quite considerably in the fifties, sixties and seventies, but apart from a series of pleasant Chicago sides on the Vee Jay label, his cause is really only supported by a small but loyal band of fans.

PHOTOGRAPH: SYLVIA PITCHER

Freddie King, one of the three Kings of the blues with Albert and B. B., but no relation to the others. He is regarded as one of the founders of modern blues guitar, and was a major influence on British rock guitarists. Much of his work leans towards rock and novelty songs, but he recorded a long series of catchy guitar instrumentals and intense blues. He died in 1976, aged 42, four years after this picture was taken at a Mississippi festival.

PHOTOGRAPH: DOUG FULTON

J. B. Lenoir was the blues singer who irritated a President. He specialized in social-commentary songs that campaigned against hunger, deprivation, poverty, racism and war with a boldness and courage rarely seen in the blues. But a song about President Eisenhower so annoyed the White House that it had to be withdrawn and re-recorded with less controversial lyrics. A unique vocalist and first rate, sensitive song writer, he was a tragic loss when a car crash in 1967 led to his death, aged just 38.

PHOTOGRAPH: BRIAN SMITH

Eddie Burns, another of the many Mississippi bluesmen, is one of those better known for his work as accompanist than as a leader. He made a few records under his own name in the late forties and fifties, but it was his tough guitar and harmonica underpinning to the then young John Lee Hooker for which he is most noted. He still records occasionally, but has never been a front rank star or a real headliner.

PHOTOGRAPH: SYLVIA PITCHER

He looks rather like Dizzy Gillespie in a thoughtful moment, but this is 'Homesick' James Williamson, cousin of Elmore James and a slide guitar player with a very effective, unschooled approach to rhythm and timing. He claims to have recorded with Little Buddy Doyle in the thirties, but his main claim to fame is a long and (until recently) largely unissued set of sides for small labels in the fifties. Despite his innovative way of playing and his continuing popularity, he remains largely in the shadow of cousin Elmore.

PHOTOGRAPH: SYLVIA PITCHER

Clarence 'Gatemouth' Brown always insists he isn't a bluesman – he's a performer of American music. And he's right. A Gatemouth album will include blues, and also country music, raging cajun, ballads, swing, rock, and anything else that takes his fancy. A skilled multi-instrumentalist, Brown has been active since the war and is still turning out records of a high standard. An adopted Texan, Brown has taken the music a long way from the basic Texas styles of Lightnin' Hopkins or T-Bone Walker.

PHOTOGRAPH: DAVE PEABODY

Lazy Lester (Leslie Johnson) was another of the evocatively named bluesmen recorded by Louisiana producer Jay Miller in the fifties and sixties. His vocals and harmonica were in the Jimmy Reed mode, and much of his best work is behind other Miller artists, such as Lightnin' Slim. His own records, like 'I'm a Lover Not A Fighter' and 'Sugar Coated Love', were great favourites with British rhythm and blues groups. Lester started a new career in 1987, and is pictured here at London's 100 Club.

PHOTOGRAPH: SYLVIA PITCHER

Rufus Thomas, the Clown Prince of the blues, recorded a long series of canine-influenced records after his big hit, 'Walking the Dog'. He started as a minstrel-show entertainer before recording for Sun, where his 'Bear Cat', an answer to Big Mama Thornton's 'Hound Dog', was a considerable success. His move to soul label Stax with his daughter Carla virtually ended his blues days until the late seventies, when he returned to his roots. He is pictured here (right) in 1991, with Lou Thimes at Radio KATZ, St Louis.

PHOTOGRAPH: BILL GREENSMITH

R. L. Burnside picked up his percussive guitar style from watching Fred McDowell play, and, like McDowell, he represents the remarkable durability of the traditional Mississippi blues. He might plug in these days, but the music he plays wouldn't be out place at a concert by Bukka White or Son House. Sadly, he didn't record until the late sixties, but since then he has toured Europe and built up a loyal following for his timeless music. He is pictured at Independence, Mississippi, in 1991.

PHOTOGRAPH: AXEL KÜSTNER

Luther Allison, pictured at London's 100 Club in 1988, started as a gospel singer, but turned to the blues in the early fifties. His guitar work is strongly influenced by Freddie King and Magic Sam, but it took a conscious move towards rock to get his career moving outside the Chicago clubs. He has recorded for enthusiasts' labels and appeared on the festival and club circuit, but never really exceeded journeyman status.

PHOTOGRAPH: DAVE PEABODY

Johnny Copeland, pictured in Bonn in 1985, was born in Louisiana, but made his name in the clubs of Houston. His early records for a succession of labels had little impact, despite his versatility and spectacular live performances. The eighties saw an upturn in his career, with two major awards for a 1986 Alligator album with Albert Collins and Robert Cray. He was the first American bluesman to record in Africa and one of the first to play behind the Iron Curtain.

PHOTOGRAPH: AXEL KÜSTNER

This extraordinary musical Christmas tree is Eddie Kirkland – his tailor and guitar designer are wisely anonymous! Jamaican-born Kirkland was an active member of the post-war Detroit blues scene, along with John Lee Hooker, Baby Boy Warren and Bobo Jenkins; but although he made a number of records under his own name, he is most highly regarded for his work backing Hooker. He remains a second-string recording artist with a reputation for first-class live shows.

PHOTOGRAPH: BILL GREENSMITH

Albert Collins was dubbed 'The Iceman', partly because of his cool, sparse, Texas guitar style, but also for a long series of records on chilly themes – 'The Freeze', 'Frosty', 'Frostbite', 'Sno-Cone', and so on. A cousin of Lightnin' Hopkins, he gained experience in the Houston clubs and recorded blues for small labels and funk-blues for the major Imperial label. His real blues legacy lies in his award-winning albums for Alligator. The Iceman died in 1994.

PHOTOGRAPH: DAVE PEABODY

An evocative picture of Big Joe Duskin, a boogie and blues player from Cincinnati, a city which had a small but thriving blues scene before the war, with artists like the Cincinnati Jug Band, and a mystery duo who seem to have recorded as Bob and Walter Coleman, and Kid and Walter Cole. Duskin has recorded little, but is a firm favourite on his European tours. One album featured Duskin with backing by guitarist Dave Peabody, who also took this 1988 photograph in Manchester, England.

PHOTOGRAPH: DAVE PEABODY

You might not know his name, but his work is a foundation of modern music. Johnny Johnson's reputation was built as a sideman rather than in his own right. In his case, it was as Chuck Berry's pianist, helping to define the sound of rock 'n' roll on dozens of influential hit records. He was with Berry for 30 years, and it wasn't until 1991 that an album with Eric Clapton and Rolling Stone Keith Richard brought him into the limelight in his own right.

PHOTOGRAPH: DAVE PEABODY

Kenny Neal, guitar, and Lucky Peterson, piano, make a
formidable duo. Neal is the son of bluesman Raful Neal,
who gave Buddy Guy his first break. Kenny also played in
his father's band, but has since cut several albums that mix
swamp blues with soul and disco rhythms to sterling effect.
In 1991 he won a theatre award in a Broadway musical.
Peterson recorded his first album at the age of five, and has
gone on to more mature, soulful albums.

PHOTOGRAPH: MARC MARNIE

Joe Louis Walker stands with Robert Cray as one of the
young lions who have rejuvenated the blues. His dynamic
guitar work echoes the wailing style of Otis Rush and
Buddy Guy, but, like Cray, he uses the tradition as a
foundation stone rather than a boundary. He has toured
and recorded widely, and is one of the most promising of
the younger players.

PHOTOGRAPH: MARC MARNIE

Taj Mahal is an impressive pseudonym – almost as impressive as his real name: Henry Saint Clair Fredericks. His first record in 1967 featured the twenties song 'I Wish I Could Shimmy Like My Sister Kate', coupled with Louis Jordan's forties hit 'Let the Good Times Roll' – an interesting start to the career of a modern-day songster who had a band with Ry Cooder and also made a reggae album. He remains indefinable, but can sing great blues when he wants to.

PHOTOGRAPH: DAVE PEABODY

The blues was becoming moribund outside specialist circles – until Robert Cray. His song-writing skills, his ability to mix traditional blues with soul and rock, and his highly versatile voice and guitar helped sell more than a million copies each of two of his albums. Every new recording shows another facet of a major talent who has used the blues as a foundation for a kind of music which appeals to a new generation – the key to the blues' survival as living music.

PHOTOGRAPH: DAVE PEABODY

index

Page numbers in italics refer
to illustrations

144